WORKBOOK

Revise
WJEC GCSE
English
Language

For Wales

Natalie Simpson

Julie Swain

Consultant:
Barry Childs

OXFORD
UNIVERSITY PRESS

OXFORD
UNIVERSITY PRESS

Great Clarendon Street, Oxford, OX2 6DP, United Kingdom

Oxford University Press is a department of the University of Oxford.

It furthers the University's objective of excellence in research, scholarship, and education by publishing worldwide. Oxford is a registered trade mark of Oxford University Press in the UK and in certain other countries

© Oxford University Press 2017

First published in 2017

British Library Cataloguing in Publication Data

Data available

ISBN 978-019-840838-3

10 9 8 7 6 5 4 3 2 1

Printed in Great Britain by CPI Group (UK) Ltd., Croydon CR0 4YY

Acknowledgements
The authors and publisher are grateful for permission to reprint extracts from the following copyright material:

Emma Barnett: 'Why we can't live without our mobile phones', The Telegraph, 16 Feb 2012, copyright © Telegraph Media Group Ltd 2012, reprinted by permission of TMG

David Black: 'Why Edinburgh should be stripped off its UNESCO World Heritage status', The Guardian, 11 Feb 2015, copyright © Guardian News & Media Ltd. 2015, 2017, reprinted by permission of GNM.

Frank Cotrell Boyce: Millions (Macmillan Children's Books, 2004), copyright © Frank Cotrell Boyce 2004, reprinted by permission of the publishers.

Ray Bradbury: 'June 2001: - And the Moon be Still as Bright', first published in Thrilling Wonder Stories, June 1948, copyright © Ray Bradbury 1948, in The Martian Chronicles (HarperVoyager, 2008) reprinted by permission of HarperCollins Publishers, Ltd.

Laura Clark: 'Children should be allowed to use mobiles in class, because they help them learn, study says', Daily Mail, 4 Sept 2008, copyright © Daily Mail 2008, reprinted by permission of Solo Syndication, for Associated Newspaper Ltd.

Lauren Davidson: 'What your home will look like when you live on Mars', The Telegraph, 7 Nov 2016, copyright © Telegraph Media Group Ltd 2016, reprinted by permission of TMG.

Steve Doughty: 'How mobiles have created a generation without manners', Daily Mail, 5 Sept 2013, copyright © Daily Mail 2013, reprinted by permission of Solo Syndication, for Associated Newspaper Ltd.

Charles Duhigg and David Barboza: 'In China, human costs are built into an i-pad', New York Times, 25 Jan 2012, The New York Times, reprinted by permission via PARS International (Syndication) and protected by the Copyright Laws of the United States. All rights reserved.

Huw Fullerton: 'The first picture for Dr Who spin-off Class is here - and it looks super dark', Radio Times, 1 Sept 2016, copyright © Radio Times immediate Media 2016, reprinted by permission of Immediate Media Syndication on behalf of the Radio Times.

Gerard Gilbert: 'Katherine Kelly interview: the former Coronation Street star on what to expect from her new Doctor Who spin-off, Class'. The Independent, 4 Oct 2016, copyright © The Independent 2015, reprinted by permission of Independent Print Ltd/ ESI Media.

Chris Hadfield: An Astronaut's Guide to Life on Earth: What Going to Space Taught Me about Ingenuity, Determination, and Being Prepared for Anything (Macmilan, 2013), copyright © Chris Hadfield 2013, reprinted by permission of Pan Macmillan via PLS Clear.

Matt Haigh: Preface to The Humans (Canongate, 2014), copyright © Matt Haigh 2014, reprinted by permission of Canongate Books Ltd.

Rin Hamburgh & Karin Simpson: 'The lost art of handwriting', The Guardian, 21 Aug 2013, copyright © Guardian News & Media Ltd 2013, 2017, reprinted by permission of GNM.

Independent Living: advice article 'Accessible holidays at home and abroad', reprinted by permission of the Editor at www.independentliving.co.uk.

Julia Llewellyn Smith: 'Staying at home is the latest holiday trend, says new survey', The Telegraph, 4 April 2009, copyright © Telegraph Media Group Ltd 2009, reprinted by permission of TMG

Mary McCarney: 'Space camp: It's out of this world', The Telegraph, 23 Nov 2014, copyright © Telegraph Media Group Ltd 2014, reprinted by permission of TMG

Ryan O'Hare: 'What will YOU be doing in 10 years?', Daily Mail, 9 Aug 2016, copyright © Pres Association 2016, reprinted by permission of the Press Association.

Graeme Paton: 'Pupils losing marks in exams due to poor handwriting', The Telegraph, 15 May 2014, copyright © Telegraph Media Group Ltd 2014, reprinted by permission of TMG

Martin Townsend: 'A word from the Editor: our children will suffer for our mobile phone addiction', Sunday Express, 18 Oct 2015, copyright © Express Newspapers 2015, reprinted by permission of Express Newspapers.

US Space & Rocket Center: 'choose your adventure', information on the Space Camp Program, 2016, reprinted by permission of the US Space & Rocket Center.

Visit Pembrokeshire: extract from Homepage (2016) at www.visitpembrokeshire.com

Although we have made every effort to trace and contact all copyright holders before publication this has not been possible in all cases. If notified, the publisher will rectify any errors or omissions at the earliest opportunity.

The publisher and authors would like to thank the following for permission to use photographs and other copyright material:

Cover: Wong Hock weng/Shutterstock; **p9:** National Space Centre; **p10:** NASA/Gary Daines; **p13:** UK Space Agency/Max Alexander/G. Zoeschinger; **p23:** Copyright © BBC Photo Library; **p27, 73:** Shutterstock; **p74:** Courtesy of Orange/EE; **p80(t):** www.teachingideas.co.uk; **p103:** Jake Lyell/Alamy Stock Photo; **p133:** David Askham/Alamy Stock Photo; **p135:** Torfaen County Borough Council; **p136:** Blaenavon World Heritage Site; **p140:** Visit Britain.

Every effort has been made to contact copyright holders of material reproduced in this book. Any omissions will be rectified in subsequent printings if notice is given to the publisher.

Contents

WJEC GCSE English Language specification overview

The exam papers

The grade you receive at the end of your WJEC GCSE English Language course is based on your performance in two exam papers and your non-examination assessment, oracy. The following provides a summary of the two exam papers:

Exam paper	Reading and Writing questions and marks	Assessment Objectives	Timing	Marks (and % of GCSE)
Unit 2: Reading and Writing: Description, Narration and Exposition	**Section A Reading:** Understanding at least one description, one narration and one exposition text, including continuous and noncontinuous texts Exam questions and marks: • Range of structured questions (35 marks) • Editing tasks (5 marks)	Reading: • AO2	2 hours	**Reading:** 40 marks (20% of GCSE) **Writing:** 40 marks (20% of GCSE)
	Section B: Writing for audience, purpose and impact: Extended writing, drawing upon texts from Section A as appropriate Exam questions and marks: • Proofreading task focusing on writing accurately (5 marks) • Choice of two writing tasks from a choice of two that could be description, narration or exposition (20 marks are awarded for communication and organization; 15 marks are awarded for writing accurately)	Writing: • AO3		**Paper 1 total:** 80 marks (40% of GCSE)
Unit 3: Reading and Writing: Argumentation, Persuasion and Instructional	**Section A Reading:** Understanding of at least one argumentation, one persuasion and one instructional text, including continuous and noncontinuous texts Exam questions and marks: • Range of structured short response and extended response questions (40 marks)	Reading: • AO2	2 hours	**Reading:** 40 marks (20% GCSE) **Writing:** 40 marks (20% GCSE)
	Section B: Writing imaginatively and creatively: Extended writing, drawing upon texts from Section A as appropriate Exam questions and marks: • One compulsory argumentation writing task (10 marks are awarded for communication and organization; 10 marks are awarded for writing accurately) • One compulsory persuasion writing task (10 marks are awarded for communication and organization; 10 marks are awarded for writing accurately)	Writing: • AO3		**Paper 2 total:** 80 marks (40% of GCSE)

How this workbook is structured

Reading

The Reading sections of this workbook take you through the requirements of each assessment objective for Section A for each of the two exam papers. As well as guidance and activities, you will also find extracts of sample student responses and examiner commentaries. There are spaces to write your answers into throughout the workbook.

Writing

The Writing sections of this workbook focus on preparing you for the types of writing you will face in Section B of each of the two exam papers. You will also find a range of strategies to help you when approaching the writing tasks as well as practice opportunities.

Sample exam papers

The workbook concludes with two full sample exam papers, one for Unit 2 and one for Unit 3.

What are the main features within this workbook?

Activities and texts

To help you practise your reading responses, you will find activities throughout this workbook all linked to the types of questions you will face in your exams. The source texts also reflect the types of texts you will be reading and responding to in your exams.

✏ **Activity 1**

Tips and Key terms

These features help support your understanding of key terms, concepts and more difficult words within a source text or exam question. These therefore enable you to concentrate fully on developing your exam response skills.

Tip

Key term

Progress check

You will find regular formative assessments in the form of Progress checks. These enable you to establish how confident you feel about what you have been learning and help you to identify areas for further practice.

Progress check

Unit 2: Section A Reading

Summary of Unit 2: Section A Reading

Unit 2: Whole paper
• 40% of total marks for GCSE English Language
• Assessment length: 2 hours
• Section A Reading
• Section B Writing
Section A
• Half of the available marks for the paper (20% of total grade)
• Time required: 1 hour
• Several texts to read
• At least one description, one narration and one exposition text
• Texts will be continuous and non-continuous
• There will be a range of structured questions with different mark tariffs
• An editing task is also included (worth 2.5% of total grade) focusing on understanding texts at word, sentence and text level

Section A of Unit 2 will test your ability to read and understand at least one description, one narration and one exposition text linked by a common theme. You will be assessed through a range of structured questions.
The varied text types and question types will require you to demonstrate different reading approaches and different skills in answering. There will be both short-response questions (for example, multiple-choice questions, short answers, sequencing tests) and extended-response questions (for example, comprehension, analysis of text, explanation). There will also be an editing task which will focus on your understanding of short passages, requiring you to analyse words, sentences and the text as a whole.

Assessment Objectives

Section A Reading of the Unit 2 exam will test your abilities in the following assessment objectives (AOs):

- Use inference and deduction skills to retrieve and analyse information.
- Synthesize and summarize information.
- Interpret themes, meaning, ideas and information.
- Edit texts and compare and evaluate usefulness, relevance and presentation of content.
- Refer to evidence within texts, distinguishing between statements that are supported by evidence and those that are not.
- Evaluate and reflect on the way in which texts may be interpreted differently according to the perspective of the reader.
- Understand and recognize the purpose and reliability of texts.

Activity 1

Based on what you have read, answer the following questions.

1. What percentage of your total marks come from the Reading section of Unit 2?

    _____

2. What do you know about the texts that you will be reading in this exam?

    _____

    _____

    _____

3. What do you know about the editing task that will be included in the Reading section?

    _____

    _____

    _____

4. How long should you spend on the Reading section of this exam?

    _____

5. How long will the Unit 2 exam take in total?

    _____

1 Different text types

Learning focus:

- To develop awareness of text types
- To revise how to approach different texts
- To explore ways to present the information you have located

In the following section you will complete activities that will help you revise how to identify text types. You will then practise how to interpret the information you are presented with.

In both Unit 2 and Unit 3 exams you will be presented with a variety of **continuous** and **non-continuous texts**. These will require different reading approaches and different types of response. Continuous text is written in sentences and paragraphs. Non-continuous text presents information in other ways; for example, charts, tables, diagrams and graphs.

Key terms

Continuous text: text written in sentences and paragraphs

Non-continuous text: text which presents information in other ways; for example, charts, tables, diagrams and graphs

Activity 1

Write down three different examples of continuous text you have come across.

- _____

- _____

- _____

Write down three different examples of non-continuous text you have come across.

- _____

- _____

- _____

The texts on pages 9 and 10 are non-continuous texts. You will be asked to retrieve information from these texts and, in some cases, to interpret or explain the information that you have found.

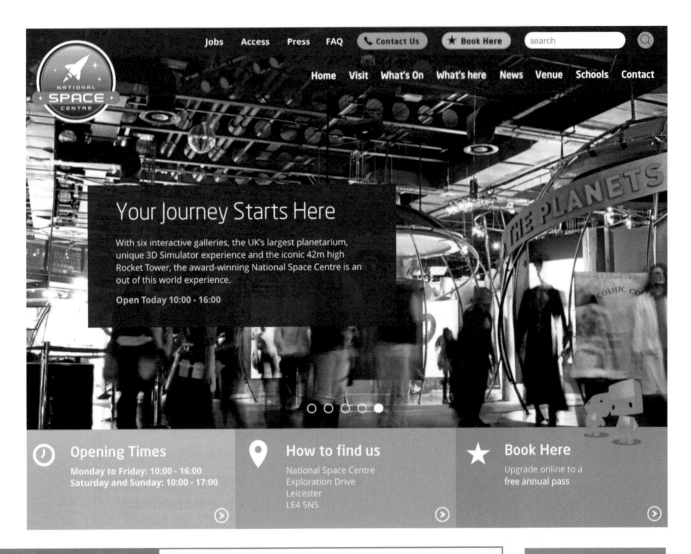

Home   Visit   What's On   What's here   News   Venue   Schools   Contact

Your Journey Starts Here

With six interactive galleries, the UK's largest planetarium, unique 3D Simulator experience and the iconic 42m high Rocket Tower, the award-winning National Space Centre is an out of this world experience.

Open Today 10:00 - 16:00

Opening Times
Monday to Friday: 10:00 - 16:00
Saturday and Sunday: 10:00 - 17:00

How to find us
National Space Centre
Exploration Drive
Leicester
LE4 5NS

Book Here
Upgrade online to a
free annual pass

✎ Activity 2

To practise your location skills, **scan** through the text above to see if you can answer the following questions:

1. What time does the National Space Centre open today?

    _____

2. What time does the National Space Centre close on a Sunday?

    _____

3. How high is the Rocket Tower?

    _____

4. What city is the National Space Centre based in?

    _____

5. How many interactive galleries are there at the National Space Centre?

    _____

Key term

Scan: a reading technique that consists of looking quickly through a text to find specific details, rather than reading it closely to take in all the information

✏ Activity 3

Look again at the line on page 9 which states 'the award-winning National Space Centre is an out of this world experience'. Explain the effect of this description and why it might persuade you to visit.

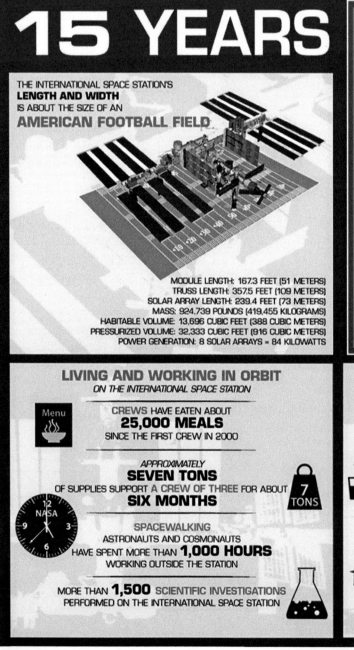

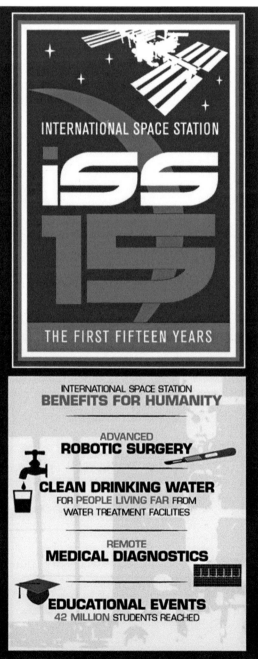

Activity 4

Look at the fact sheet on page 10 which presents information on the first 15 years of the International Space Station. Answer the following questions:

1. What are three of the ways in which humans have benefited from the International Space Station?

    • _____

    • _____

    • _____

2. List three facts you have learned about life in orbit.

    • _____

    • _____

    • _____

Activity 5

Write down three questions you might be asked to prompt you to locate information in this text. Each question should be worth one mark.

• _____
_____
_____
_____

• _____
_____
_____
_____

• _____
_____
_____
_____

Tip

If you are given bullet point spaces for your answer in an exam, make sure you set your answer out using the bullet points. Do not put more than one answer in one bullet point space.

2 Multiple-choice questions

Learning focus:

- To develop awareness of how multiple-choice questions might be used
- To explore types of multiple-choice question
- To think about ways to approach multiple-choice questions

You will be asked three multiple-choice questions in the Reading sections of the exams for Unit 2 and Unit 3. These will test a combination of different skills including your ability to:

- locate information
- deduce word meaning
- use verbal reasoning skills
- understand texts in **context**
- show awareness of the purpose of text.

No matter what multiple-choice question you are set, it is essential that you read the area of text that it refers to very carefully. The context of what you read is often very important when answering a multiple-choice question as it can help you to narrow down the choices you are presented with.

There is only one correct answer to a multiple-choice question. The other answers are called distractors. Some of the distractors will be more obviously wrong than others, so if you are not certain of the answer you may find it helpful to discount the ones that you know are wrong first to help you decide on the right answer.

> **Key term**
>
> **Context:** the words that come before and after a particular word or phrase and help clarify its meaning; the circumstances or background against which something happens

CAREERS in SPACE

UK SPACE AGENCY

If you thought a space career was all about astronauts – think again! You are already USING space every day.

The UK space sector employs over 34,000 people and is growing fast – aiming for 100,000 new jobs by 2030.

Credit: Max Alexander – UK Space Agency

Credit: G. Zoeschinger

Engineers – mechanical and electrical; technicians and graduates; working together to design and build spacecraft, robots and sensors

Computer Scientists, Mathematicians, Software and System Designers – control and monitor spacecraft; use data from space to model complex systems in Earth, navigation or communications science

Natural Scientists – use physics, chemistry, biology, Earth and atmospheric sciences to design sensors and use data models to learn more about the planet, ourselves and the Universe.

Applications developers – 75% of 'space jobs' are in companies using space to derive and deliver information, products and services to the public – from agriculture to disaster response, from logistics to communications, insurance to exploration for natural resources.

Activity 1

Look at the poster on page 13, then answer the following multiple-choice questions.

1. Which of the following 'space jobs' is explained in this poster?

    a. Administrator ☐

    b. Robot ☐

    c. Mathematician ☐

    d. Astronaut ☐

2. The poster refers to companies which use space 'to derive and deliver information, products and services to the public'. Select one definition from the list below which best explains this:

    a. Companies that use space knowledge to create and pass on additional services ☐

    b. Companies that deliver their products through space ☐

    c. Companies that are able to gain helpful knowledge from space ☐

    d. Companies that use space knowledge to prevent disasters ☐

3. Which of the following statements about jobs in the space sector is not true?

    a. The UK space sector is growing quickly. ☐

    b. Engineers are employed to design and build spacecraft. ☐

    c. 75% of 'space jobs' are in the field of application development. ☐

    d. Natural scientists use data from space to develop navigation systems. ☐

    e. The UK space sector is aiming to provide 100,000 new jobs by 2030. ☐

Check the correct answers to the questions in Activity 1 with your teacher.

If any of your answers were incorrect, have another look and see if you can work out where you went wrong.

Tip

Real care is needed when marking down your answer to multiple-choice questions. If there is any doubt about which answer you have selected, you will not be given the mark. Be sure of your answer before you make a mark on the paper. If for any reason you change your mind, make sure any changes are very clear to the examiner.

What will YOU be doing in 10 years? From biohacker to space tour guide, report predicts the jobs of the future

By PRESS ASSOCIATION and RYAN O'HARE FOR MAILONLINE

The current generation of students could choose to take up a career in designing human bodies or taking tourists around our galactic neighbourhood, according to a new report. Only a third of university students believe their chosen career will exist in 10 years' time, say Microsoft and The Future Laboratory, which produced 'Tomorrow's jobs'.

The report predicts virtual reality design, robotic engineering and visual communications will be among the jobs of the future. 'While these jobs may seem like the realms of science fiction, in reality they are indicative of changes that we are already seeing today,' said Microsoft's Ryan Asdourian. [...]

The research predicts that almost two-thirds of school students today will end up working in jobs which do not yet exist, with the report forming part of efforts to prepare for the roles and the skills needed.

Steve Tooze, of The Future Laboratory, said: 'Technological change, economic turbulence and societal transformation are disrupting old career certainties, making it increasingly difficult to judge which degrees and qualifications will remain a passport to a well-paid and fulfilling job in the decades ahead.'

Among the jobs yet to be created include space tour guide. But companies such as Virgin Galactic and Blue Origin plan on taking passengers into suborbital space, and those intrepid explorers aboard the new wave of passenger craft will need a guide.

JOBS OF THE FUTURE

Virtual Habitat Designer: The report predicts that millions of people will work and learn in virtual environments in the future, opening up the field to designers to create these new worlds.

Ethical Technology Advocate: How we interact with robots, the regulation of self-driving cars, the use of artificial intelligence in warfare and even in insurance profiling will all require ethical guidance, creating new fields of expertise.

Rewilding Strategist: While many species may be dwindling, environmentalists are looking to reintroduce native species such as wolves and elk to regions where they have been wiped out – which will take considerable conservation planning.

Freelance Biohacker: We have already seen biohackers implant themselves with microchips and even try to give themselves night vision, but open source publishing, software and tools could enable anyone to participate.

Internet of Things (IoT) Data Creative: With everything from your fridge to your toothbrush set to become connected via the IoT, people will need to analyse the data collected to work out what's useful and what trends appear.

Activity 2

Read the article on page 15 on jobs of the future and answer the following questions:

1. Microsoft's Ryan Asdourian refers to predicted future jobs as 'indicative of changes' that we are already seeing. Select one definition that best defines 'indicative'.

   a. A collection of details ☐

   b. Serving as a sign ☐

   c. Multiple reasons ☐

   d. Not typical ☐

2. According to the research in the report, which of the following is not offered as a prediction for the future?

   a. Millions of people will work and/or learn in virtual environments. ☐

   b. Two thirds of today's school children will end up working in jobs that currently don't exist. ☐

   c. Biohackers will implant themselves with microchips. ☐

   d. Jobs yet to be created include space tour guide and designers of human bodies. ☐

In working out the correct answer to a multiple-choice question, **verbal reasoning** skills are needed. If you are not sure of the answer, re-read the question and the text to see if looking at the context helps you and then think carefully about the answers you are presented with.

Key term

Verbal reasoning: skills which help you understand and comprehend information, like reason and deduction

Activity 3

Write two of your own multiple-choice questions based on this article. Think about the way you use the distractors – they must seem like credible alternatives and require the person answering to think carefully about why they are not the correct choice.

- --

- --

  ----

3 Decoding questions

Learning focus:

- To understand what a question is asking
- To provide focus on questions worth a higher number of marks

It is essential that you understand exactly what a question is asking you to do before you attempt to answer it. Too many students set off thinking they know what they are doing and come unstuck before the end as they realize that their answer does not quite match the task. Read carefully the following steps to take before starting to write your answer.

1. Read the question carefully.

2. Double check you know exactly which text (or texts) you are supposed to be looking at. If the focus is a specific area of a text, put a line next to the start and end point to remind you of the area you need to look at.

3. Re-read the question and underline any key terms. This will help you to understand what you are being asked to do.

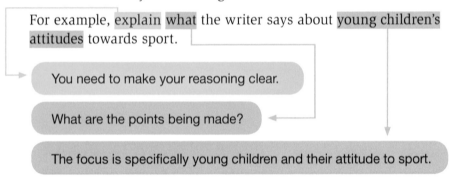

For example, explain what the writer says about young children's attitudes towards sport.

You need to make your reasoning clear.

What are the points being made?

The focus is specifically young children and their attitude to sport.

4. Read the text and highlight any evidence that will help you to answer the question.

5. Re-read the question once more before beginning your answer.

Read the question below and the text to which it relates.

Read Text A.

Explain why space travel may soon become a possibility for more people.
[5]

Text A

2016 Could Be the Year Space Tourism Takes Off

Suborbital rocket flights may soon be available to people who are merely really rich.

By Taylor Dinerman

Until now Space Tourism meant very very rich people paying very large sums of money to ride Russian rockets on relatively short trips to the International Space Station (ISS). [...]

Meanwhile another form of Space Tourism, suborbital rocket flights, may soon be available. [...] People who are merely really rich will be able to buy rides into space. As traditionally defined space begins 50 kilometres above the Earth's surface, thus a rocket that takes passengers to that altitude or beyond is taking them into space. Even without going into orbit, the new Space Tourists will not only experience weightlessness, but will look down on Earth from space, a view that all who've seen it concur is one of the most beautiful and amazing things they've ever seen.

Virgin Galactic, a spin off from Richard Branson's Virgin group, is building a new copy of the Space Ship Two (SS2) design after the first one crashed near Mojave California last year killing one crew member and injuring the other. [...] In operation, Virgin Galactic will hang Space Ship Two with its pilots and six passengers underneath the White Knight carrier aircraft which will fly to roughly 40,000 feet and release the rocket-plane. Once free of the carrier, SS2 will light its hybrid rocket engine and zoom to an altitude of more than 100 kilometres, where passengers will experience "Several minutes" of weightlessness before strapping back into their seats for the ride back to Earth.

Virgin Galactic CEO George Whitesides is confident that the firm will resume flight testing within "months." He hopes that after flight testing has been completed at Mojave [...] the company will then begin taking some of the roughly 700 customers who've already signed up, into space. According to Mr. Whitesides, fewer than 30 existing customers cancelled their plans after the accident last year.

Meanwhile VG's competition is making progress. Xcor Aerospace, based, at least for now, in Mojave, is steadily working away on their Lynx two-seat rocket-plane. This craft is designed to take off directly from a runway and blast its way to 200,000 ft altitude, and then glide back to Earth. Each flight will carry a pilot and one paying passenger who will be charged a little less than $100,000 for the trip. Xcor soon hopes to be able to fly more than twice daily. [...]

In any case the Space Tourism industry and the New Space Industry as a whole have survived the great recession and are emerging as small, but important players in the US aerospace industry. If the US and the world economy soars in the next few years, the market for rides into space will just keep growing. [...]

As Space Tourism grows, trips will be limited to people who are both wealthy and healthy, but, as with any new industry, eventually the experience will be affordable by the broad middle class. As of now less than six hundred humans have flown into space, sometime soon expect that number to increase dramatically. When millions of ordinary people have friends or relations who've gone into space, will humanity look out into space with the same awe and wonder that we now do? Perhaps people will come to view the Moon, Mars and the rest of the Solar System as just part of our neighbourhood?

✎ Activity 1

Neither of the following answers to this exam question scored highly. Can you explain why?

Answer 1

Space travel might become a possibility because not just rich people will be able to afford it. It will be cheaper and people will come to think of the moon and all the planets as places to travel to. More people will be able to 'experience weightlessness, but will look down on Earth from space'. Richard Branson will be flying his galactic aeroplanes to space and he will want more people to buy tickets to go to space.

This answer did not score highly because:

_____

_____

_____

_____

_____

Answer 2

- 'People who are merely really rich will be able to buy rides into space'
- 'Virgin Galactic, a spin off from Richard Branson's Virgin group, is building a new copy of the Space Ship Two'
- 'Virgin Galactic CEO George Whitesides is confident that the firm will resume flight testing within "months."'
- 'Xcor Aerospace, based, at least for now, in Mojave, is steadily working away on their Lynx two-seat rocket-plane.'
- 'Xcor soon hopes to be able to fly more than twice daily.'

This answer did not score highly because:

_____

_____

_____

_____

_____

Activity 2

Now re-read the following question:

> Read Text A.
>
> Explain why space travel may soon become a possibility for more people. **[5]**

1. Annotate the question using the steps suggested at the beginning of this lesson. Try to avoid the mistakes that you have seen made in the answers on page 19 and focus on what you are being asked to do.

2. Answer the question on the lines below.

----

4 Using evidence

Learning focus:

- To look at how to use evidence within an exam answer
- To demonstrate how to set out evidence within an answer

You must choose evidence carefully in order to show how closely you have read a text as well as to demonstrate the clear focus of your answer. Try to avoid quoting huge chunks of text – this does not demonstrate your ability to select carefully. The best evidence is generally quite short and directly relevant to the question you have been asked and the point you are making.

The following is taken from an interview with Katherine Kelly on 'what to expect from her new *Doctor Who* spin-off, *Class*'.

In *Class*, set in Coal Hill, a fictional school that has featured in *Doctor Who* since its inception in 1963, Kelly plays the physics teacher, Miss Quill – "the teacher that you would just never want", says Kelly. "She is more intelligent than all of the kids put together and she cannot bear them and she's very happy to dole out detention. But if you were ever in serious trouble, she would be the one you go to because she's totally kick-ass. She's a bit of a dream role, really."

Produced by Steven Moffat and written by Patrick Ness, an American author best-known for his books for young adults, the series concentrates on the secrets and desires of the academy's sixth-formers – with added monsters.

"It's very much part of the *Doctor Who* family – Peter Capaldi's in the first episode – and we are fighting aliens left, right and centre, so there was a lot of green screen and typical sci-fi filming," says Kelly. "When I told my dad about *Class*, and that I was going to play Miss Quill and I was describing it all, he said, 'that means you can never be the first female Doctor Who'."

Activity 1

In the table below, a number of points have been made about this interview. Select evidence which could be used to support these points.

Idea	Evidence
Coal Hill is a school that has always been part of the *Doctor Who* universe.	
Miss Quill is an interesting teacher to play.	
Patrick Ness has experience of writing for this audience.	
Coal Hill is a typical school in some ways.	
Katherine Kelly's father may have been disappointed.	

The first picture for *Doctor Who* spin-off *Class* is here, and it looks super dark

By Huw Fullerton

The first picture for long-awaited *Doctor Who* spin-off *Class* has arrived, and it's definitely looking like the darker take on the Whoniverse that series creator Patrick Ness promised when the series was first announced last year.

The image shows Katherine Kelly's mysterious Miss Quill standing with student April (Sophie Hopkins) in the hallway of Coal Hill School, apparently at night. April is aiming an alien weapon at an unseen threat, while Quill (described as a "powerful new presence" in the original casting announcement) offers some kind of warning or encouragement.

Of course, due to the little we know about the series there's very little we can tell about what's going on in the picture. It could be that it hints at Hopkins being the alien lead character referenced in earlier press releases given her gun, or that Kelly's character is on the side of the young heroes given her position with April.

Alternatively it could mean the complete opposite of those things depending on the context of the episode, so we really still don't have much to go on until some kind of trailer is finally released.

Still, it does seem like one detail is confirmed – this picture makes *Class* look like a slightly scarier, more serious take on the world of *Doctor Who*, and we simply can't wait to see what that's like. The next month can't pass quickly enough.

Activity 2

How does Huw Fullerton create excitement towards the new television series 'Class'?   [5]

1. Using the advice you read in the previous lesson underline the key words in this question.

2. Two pieces of evidence you may consider using as part of an answer to this question have already been highlighted for you. Can you highlight any additional evidence?

3. Complete the table below to show what you could write about your evidence selection.

Evidence	How does this create excitement?
'long-awaited Doctor Who spin-off'	The writer immediately makes it sound like this series has been anticipated for some time and that he knows that his readers have been waiting impatiently.
'the darker take... Patrick Ness promised'	The fact that the series creator has made promises to fans suggests that he seems to have delivered what people wanted from this series.

When you use evidence in your answer it should be integrated (or woven in) as part of your explanation. For example, an answer to the exam question on page 24 could begin:

> Fullerton creates excitement by suggesting that there is really enthusiastic anticipation for this Doctor Who 'spin-off' series as it is 'long-awaited'.

In an exam you will not have much time to get your answer down and you need to build on what you say and the evidence you use. Try to avoid repeating yourself. Make your point and link it quickly and clearly to relevant evidence.

This is a longer and less efficient way of making the point:

> The writer, Huw Fullerton, creates excitement towards the new television series Class by making it sound like it has been anticipated for some time:
>
> 'long-awaited Doctor Who spin-off'
>
> This suggests that fans have been waiting impatiently and are keen to see the new series.

Although both answers are right, the first approach deals with the material much more efficiently and clearly.

✏ Activity 3

Using evidence you have found, complete the answer to the question given in the Activity 2. Try to be as direct as possible.

_____

_____

_____

_____

_____

_____

_____

_____

_____

Tip

Use phrases like 'this suggests' or 'this implies' to make it clear that you are making a point about the language used by the writer. Your answer will become more focused as a result.

5 Synthesis

Learning focus:

- To revise the term 'synthesis'
- To practise synthesizing information from more than one text

The texts that you read in the exams will be thematically linked. You may be asked on either the Unit 2 or Unit 3 exam to **synthesize** the information that you have read from two or more texts. This means that you must draw upon material from all the specified texts to create new material that answers whatever question you have been asked.

Read the following texts about NASA's Space Camp.

> **Key term**
>
> **Synthesize:** to form something by bringing together information from different sources

Text A

Space camp: it's out of this world

Teacher Mary McCarney is over the moon after taking a group of pupils to Nasa's Space Camp

Greetings from Space Camp, the final frontier. First of all, let me apologise in advance for the numerous space clichés, although having boldly gone on the ultimate school trip with 73 fired-up, fanatical nine and 10-year-olds, I think I'm allowed a little starry-eyed indulgence. And the odd Captain Kirk misquote is pretty much inevitable.

My pupils and I spent three days at the US Space & Rocket Center in Huntsville, Alabama, joining 20,000 visitors from all over the world enrolled in Space Camp this year (including 230 pupils from the UK).

My students had a blast exploring genuine Saturn rockets, dressing up in space suits and taking part in a simulated shuttle mission, all at warp speed pace. Engaging with real-life applications of science, maths, technology and engineering, this is astronaut training for nine-year-olds. [...]

On arrival, we were greeted with a sign proclaiming, "Through these doors enter the world's future astronauts, scientists and engineers". No pressure then.

We soon began to notice we'd left civilian life on Earth behind: drinking fountains are labelled H2O Rehydration Units, stuffing your face with moon pies in the Crew Galley may involve a trip to Sick Bay, and going to the loo here means visiting the Waste Management Station.

Our school group, accompanied by myself and 10 other teachers, was reorganised into teams, each named after a famous astronaut. I found myself in Team Ride (Sally Ride was the first American woman in space), and our crew trainer was a very nice young man called Chad.

Chad launched us straight into the flight simulators. These included the multi-axis trainer, which replicates tumbling manoeuvres in space to help acclimatise astronauts for disorientation. Resembling a giant gyroscope, it whirled my strapped-in students in every direction imaginable, and amazingly no one puked up their lunch. [...]

Day two kicked off with the highlight of our trip — a simulated shuttle mission. The kids quickly got the hang of the acronym-laden lingo, and each child was assigned a specific job and detailed responsibilities. [...] This was a great team-building, leadership and decision-making exercise, which they thoroughly enjoyed.

Our three days at camp included learning lots of space history too. We watched Imax movies and completed educational assignments inside the museum. My students were fascinated by the exhibition about animals in space, featuring the two famous American monkeynauts, Able and Baker. [...]

Our trip culminated in a special graduation ceremony for us new space cadets. We were treated to an inspirational speech by Col Marks, the garrison commander of Redstone Arsenal.

We were following in giant footsteps, he told us: several former graduates of Space Camp have grown up to become Nasa astronauts. [...]

As school trips go, this has to be the highlight of my 26-year teaching career on both sides of the Atlantic. For aspiring astronauts, children (or teachers) who want to reach for the stars, or any child who loves astronomy, the Space Camp experience is out of this world. Sorry; just couldn't resist that one…

Mary McCarney is an English teacher at Atlanta International School, USA

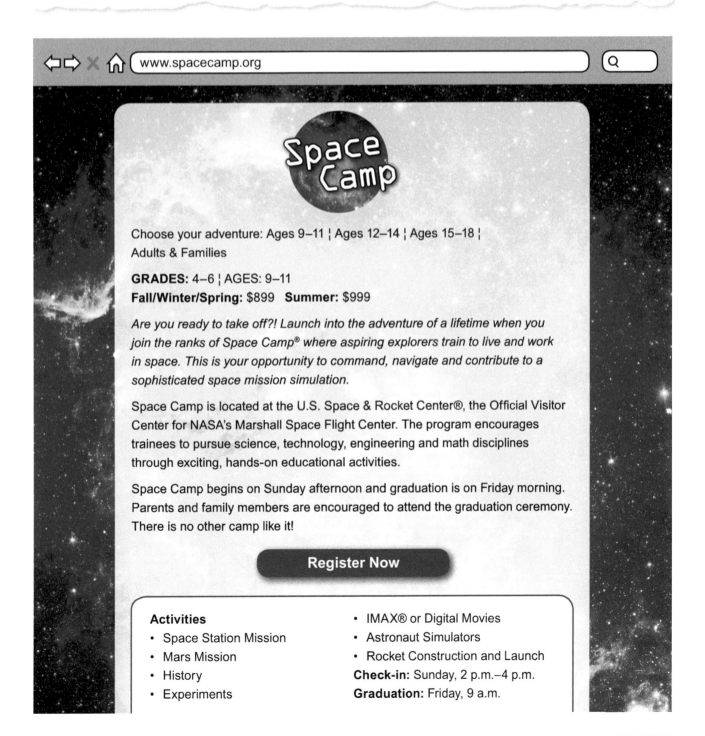

www.spacecamp.org

Space Camp

Choose your adventure: Ages 9–11 ¦ Ages 12–14 ¦ Ages 15–18 ¦ Adults & Families

GRADES: 4–6 ¦ **AGES:** 9–11
Fall/Winter/Spring: $899   **Summer:** $999

Are you ready to take off?! Launch into the adventure of a lifetime when you join the ranks of Space Camp® where aspiring explorers train to live and work in space. This is your opportunity to command, navigate and contribute to a sophisticated space mission simulation.

Space Camp is located at the U.S. Space & Rocket Center®, the Official Visitor Center for NASA's Marshall Space Flight Center. The program encourages trainees to pursue science, technology, engineering and math disciplines through exciting, hands-on educational activities.

Space Camp begins on Sunday afternoon and graduation is on Friday morning. Parents and family members are encouraged to attend the graduation ceremony. There is no other camp like it!

Register Now

Activities
- Space Station Mission
- Mars Mission
- History
- Experiments

- IMAX® or Digital Movies
- Astronaut Simulators
- Rocket Construction and Launch

Check-in: Sunday, 2 p.m.–4 p.m.
Graduation: Friday, 9 a.m.

Although some of these texts may be a little longer than the ones you are likely to be presented with in an exam, they will provide you with extended practice of the skills that you need.

Activity 1

Complete the table below to enable you to answer the following question:

Synthesize what you learn about NASA's Space Camp in Texts A and B? **[10]**

Point	Text A	Text B
It is well attended.	'joining 20,000 visitors from all over the world enrolled in Space Camp this year'	
There are many exciting and inspiring futuristic activities.	'exploring genuine Saturn rockets, dressing up in space suits and taking part in a simulated shuttle mission, all at warp speed pace'	e.g. astronaut simulation, rocket construction and launch

Tips

- Highlight each piece of relevant evidence as you read these texts.
- Use the table to identify any common facts that you learn.
- Remember that some of the details you learn may come from **inferences** you make based on what you have read.
- Bring the information together economically.

Key term

Inference: a conclusion you reach based on evidence and reasoning

Some of the details that you learn about Space Camp will be available in both texts whereas other details will only come from one text. Read the following tips:

1. Present what you have learned and make sure that you use information from both texts.

2. Put forward your findings in a clear and concise way.

3. Use direct evidence from the text when it helps you to do so, but keep in mind that you can summarize or state what you have learned for this question.

Activity 2

Complete the answer below to the following question:

> Synthesise what you learn about NASA's Space Camp in Texts A and B? **[10]**

NASA's Space Camp is well attended with over 20,000 visitors each year. Both texts make it clear that there are many exciting and futuristic activities for children to take part in such as 'exploring genuine Saturn rockets' and 'taking part in a simulated shuttle mission'. The second text provides a list of activities including 'rocket construction and launch'.

6 Extended answers

Learning focus:

- To think about the number of marks available for a question
- To practise exploring detail in questions worth a higher number of marks

In the exams you will need to look at how many marks a question is worth. If a question is worth one or two marks, then it is sensible to assume you will need to produce a shorter answer and spend less time on it than a question that is worth ten marks.

When answering a question which is worth more marks; make sure that you are covering a range of points and that you are explaining the evidence that you put forward.

The following extract is taken from a book called *The Humans* by Matt Haigh. It is written from the perspective of an alien who has temporarily taken the form of Professor Andrew Martin in order to fulfil a mission for his own species.

Text A

I know that some of you reading this are convinced humans are a myth, but I am here to state that they do actually exist. For those that don't know, a human is a real bipedal lifeform of a mid-range intelligence, living a largely deluded existence on a small water-logged planet in a very lonely corner of the universe.

For the rest of you, and those who sent me, humans are in many respects exactly as strange as you would expect them to be. Certainly it is true that on a first sighting you would be appalled by their physical appearance.

Their faces alone contain all manner of hideous curiosities. A protuberant central nose, thin-skinned lips, primitive external auditory organs known as 'ears', tiny eyes and unfathomably pointless eyebrows. All of which take a long time to mentally absorb and accept.

The manners and social customs too are a baffling enigma at first. Their conversation topics are very rarely the things they want to be talking about, and I could write ninety-seven books on body shame and clothing etiquette before you would get even close to understanding them.

Oh, and let's not forget The Things They Do To Make Themselves Happy That Actually Make Them Miserable. This is an infinite list. It includes – shopping, watching TV, taking the better job, getting the bigger house, writing a semi-autobiographical novel, educating their young, making their skin look mildly less old, and harbouring a vague desire to believe there might be a meaning to it all.

Read Text A and think about the following question:

> What impressions does this writer give about humans?   **[5]**

Read the sample answer and teacher comment below:

Student answer

The writer creates the impressions that humans are strange to the point where some of his readers think they are a myth. ✓ He makes human life sound unpleasant and that we live 'on a small water-logged planet in a very lonely part of the universe'. ✓ He thinks that the physical appearance of a human is appalling, their faces have 'hideous curiosities'. ✓ There is lots of evidence that humans are strange, for example 'their conversation topics are very rarely the things they want to be talking about'.

Teacher comment

This is a reasonable answer that makes straightforward comments about a number of examples. Selection of detail is reasonable and directed towards the question. The answer is not as selective as it might be, though, and ignores some important evidence, which means it misses the chance to make a range of accurate points. The impression of humans being strange at the end is repeated from the opening sentence without any further development being made.

✏ Activity 1

Below is the beginning of a more detailed answer. Complete this answer using at least three of the following impressions. You will need to find and investigate evidence to support these impressions:

- Humans are not attractive.
- Their behaviour is difficult to understand.
- They do not know what is best for them.
- There are a multitude of ways in which they make themselves unhappy.

Student answer

Humans are presented as an almost myth-like curiosity in this extract. We get the impression they are not particularly bright, 'of a mid-range intelligence,' and that this may be most evident in the way they think of themselves. They are described as living a 'largely deluded existence' which suggests they are mistaken or deceived in their views of themselves and possibly their own importance.

_____

_____

_____

_____

_____

_____

Activity 2

Now test your ability to answer an extended question on your own. Don't forget to think about what the question is asking you.

1. Highlight or underline the key words in the question.

2. Read the text and highlight any evidence that will help you to answer the question.

3. Re-read the question once more before beginning your answer.

4. Write your answer as clearly as you can.

It was so cold when they first came from the rocket into the night that Spender began to gather the dry Martian wood and build a small fire. He didn't say anything about a celebration; he merely gathered the wood, set fire to it, and watched it burn.

In the flare that lighted the thin air of this dried-up sea of Mars he looked over his shoulder and saw the rocket that had brought them all, Captain Wilder and Cheroke and Hathaway and Sam Parkhill and himself, across a silent black space of stars to land upon a dead, dreaming world.

Jeff Spender waited for the noise. He watched the other men and waited for them to jump around and shout. It would happen as soon as the numbness of being 'first' men to Mars wore off. None of them said anything, but many of them were hoping, perhaps, that the other expeditions had failed and that this, the Fourth, would be the one. They meant nothing evil by it. But they stood thinking it, nevertheless, thinking of the honour and fame, while their lungs became accustomed to the thinness of the atmosphere, which almost made you drunk if you moved too quickly. [...]

He fed the fire by hand, and it was like an offering to a dead giant. They had landed on an immense tomb. Here a civilization had died. It was only simple courtesy that the first night be spent quietly. [...]

> What impressions do you have of the mood of the explorers in this extract? **[5]**

7 Evaluation

Learning focus:

- To explore ways to **evaluate** texts critically
- To revise techniques for personal response
- To focus on supporting ideas with textual references

You will be required to demonstrate the ability to evaluate in your exams. If you are asked to evaluate something, you will need to show that you can assess what you have been reading and come to a sensible judgement about it. This means you will need to think about the subject of the text and how this makes you feel. To really demonstrate your skills you need to show how the writer led you to that judgement.

In the following text, Chris Hadfield writes about the effect that watching Neil Armstrong's first steps on the moon had on him as a boy.

> **Key term**
>
> **Evaluate:** to form an idea of the state or value of something

At that moment, I knew what I wanted to do with my life. I was going to follow in the footsteps so boldly imprinted just moments before. Roaring around in a rocket, exploring space, pushing the boundaries of knowledge and human capability – I knew, with absolute clarity, that I wanted to be an astronaut.

I also knew, as did every kid in Canada, that it was impossible. Astronauts were American. NASA only accepted applications from U.S. citizens, and Canada didn't even have a space agency. But… just the day before, it had been impossible to walk on the moon. Neil Armstrong hadn't let that stop him. Maybe someday it would be possible for me to go too, and if that day ever came, I wanted to be ready. […]

I didn't announce to my parents or my brothers and sisters that I wanted to be an astronaut. That would've elicited approximately the same reaction as announcing that I wanted to be a movie star. But from that night forward, my dream provided direction to my life. I recognized even as a 9-year-old that I had a lot of choices and my decisions mattered. What I did each day would determine the kind of person I'd become.

✏ Activity 1

Think about how you react to the author's language and complete the following steps:

1. Make a list of different words you would use to describe Chris Hadfield in this extract.

2. Link each of these words to a short piece of evidence from the text.

Chosen words	Evidence
_____	_____
_____	_____
_____	_____
_____	_____
_____	_____

> **Tip**
>
> To evaluate a text critically you need to:
> - look at specific detail
> - examine evidence
> - show how you have come to a judgement by linking these together.

Activity 2

Using the notes you have just made, answer the following question. Try to keep the question in your mind and not repeat any thoughts or feelings.

> What do you think and feel about Chris Hadfield and his future plans? Use evidence from the text to support your answer. **[5]**

Activity 3

Read the passage on page 35 carefully and complete the following tasks:

1. A confident evaluation will have a clear view of the text as a whole. In no more than three sentences write down what this article is about.

2. Highlight any words or phrases in the text which may influence your opinion of life on Mars. Think about how the writer does this and annotate the text to show your ideas.

What your home will look like when you live on Mars

PROPERTY EDITOR

Put those retirement plans on hold. There's a chance that, sooner or later, you might have to move further than you were thinking. As far as Mars.

On Thursday, to mark the launch of its new six-part docudrama *Mars*, National Geographic will unveil the first ever Mars showhome, giving earthlings an idea of what their life could look like on the Red Planet.

Set in the not-so-distant year of 2037, in Valles Marineris, a vast system of canyons on the Mars equator, the igloo-shaped structure could be the home of your future.

It depicts a house built using recycled spacecraft parts and Martian soil, called regolith, which has been microwaved into bricks. Some parts of the home are recognisable – kitchen, bedroom – but there are core differences that are vital for human survival.

As the Martian atmosphere is around one hundredth as thick as the Earth's, people will need permanent shielding from the sun; society will move largely indoors. Most buildings will be connected by underground tunnels and the houses won't have windows. The homes will have simulated solar lighting, or natural light that has been refracted several times.

Walls will need to be 10 to 12ft thick, to protect people from dangerous cosmic rays that can pass through six feet of steel, and a double air-locked entrance will keep the home pressurised.

"We don't think of our houses as things that keep us alive, but on Mars your dwelling will be a survival centre," says Stephen Petranek, author of *How We'll Live on Mars* and a consultant on *Mars*. This is not just the stuff of sci-fi. "Ten to 20 years from now there will certainly be people on Mars," Petranek says.

Entrepreneur Elon Musk aims to land people on Mars by 2024 and thinks he can send 80,000 people to the Red Planet by 2050. Amazon founder Jeff Bezos is working on a similar plan.

[…]

Petranek is optimistic about humans' future on Mars. He likens the challenges of starting a new society in space to troops in war, who become close because they are dependent on each other for survival.

"I think we will create a very liveable and likeable environment," he says. "It's not terrifying. It's kind of glorious."

Mars premieres on National Geographic on Sunday November 13 at 9pm

Activity 4

Answer the following question:

> What do you think and feel about the way life on Mars is presented in this article? **[10]**

Stretch

Remind yourself of what the word 'evaluate' means before you answer the question in Activity 4. Think of any different ways this question could have been asked.

8 Editing

Learning focus:

- To revise techniques for the editing section of Unit 2
- To practise editing activities

In the Unit 2 exam you will be asked to complete some editing tasks. These will test your ability to understand short texts at word, sentence and text level. The questions will be multiple choice so you will need to use your verbal reasoning skills to work out which of the answers is the correct one.

When answering word-level questions, you will need to demonstrate understanding of the meaning of words and how they work in the context they are written in. Often it is the context (what comes before and after) which decides whether the word in question is the correct one.

✏ Activity 1

Try to answer the following:

1. I reached the (1) _____ and gazed at the view beyond. My (2) _____ was soon forgotten, adrenaline and excitement at what I had achieved took over.

    a. Circle the word that best fits gap (1):

    A) summit   B) field   C) mountain   D) bottom

    b. Circle the word that best fits gap (2):

    A) wish   B) exhaustion   C) trek   D) wound

2. Initially, the boys were (1) _____ for position on the start line but their attention was soon (2) _____ by the man holding the pistol in the air.

    a. Circle the word that best fits gap (1):

    A) jumping   B) huddling   C) jostling   D) running

    b. Circle the word that best fits gap (2):

    A) moving   B) commanded   C) devoted   D) given

3. The teacher was (1) _____ with the quality of work produced by his GCSE students. He intended to use it to (2) _____ prospective parents at the open evening.

    a. Circle the word that best fits gap (1):

    A) happy   B) delighted   C) content   D) appalled

    b. Circle the word that best fits gap (2):

    A) impress   B) entertain   C) please   D) show

✎ Activity 2

Thinking through how these types of question work can be beneficial. Imagine you are a teacher who needs to set some of these practice questions for a class. Use the space below to write two more of these questions.

• _____

   _____

   _____

   _____

   _____

   _____

   _____

• _____

   _____

   _____

   _____

   _____

   _____

Sentence-level questions also test your ability to read in context. Look at the following sample question, then try to answer some of the practice questions.

Circle the pair of words that best fit the meaning of the sentence below:

I was _____ to see the old house again; yet as I stood there a growing sense of _____ crept up on me.

A. scared ... fear

B. overjoyed ... anxiety

C. pleased ... happiness

D. horrified ... generosity

E. embarrassed ... shame

The correct answer is B.

The sentence should read: I was overjoyed to see the old house again; yet as I stood there a growing sense of anxiety crept up on me.

The word 'yet' signals that there was a change in the mood of the writer and options A, C and E do not recognize that change. Option D does not make sense in the context of this question.

Activity 3

Answer the following questions:

1. The prospect of starting a new school was_____
    for Molly, although she was _____ to get it over and done with now.

    a. daunting … keen ☐

    b. pleasing … happy ☐

    c. frightening … scared ☐

    d. uneasy … delighted ☐

    e. sickening … free ☐

2. As a result of the _____ weather, the football match
    had been _____ until further notice.

    a. poor … played ☐

    b. good … cancelled ☐

    c. extreme … postponed ☐

    d. chaotic … booked ☐

    e. inclement … removed ☐

The next questions are set out a little differently but test the same skills.

3. As a result of his recent pay rise, Owen…

    a. would be unhappy for some time now ☐

    b. knew that he could afford to treat his friends to lunch ☐

    c. decided to complain to his boss ☐

    d. demanded they split the bill equally ☐

4. Without his parents' help and support, Michael…

    a. was sure that he would succeed ☐

    b. had the best chance of achieving his dreams ☐

    c. would have struggled to recover from his accident ☐

    d. didn't want to think ☐

Activity 4

Text-level questions will ask you to think about how the text works as a whole piece.

The sentences below are from a blog about attending a football match. Put them in the right order to create a meaningful paragraph:

1. We found our seats and awaited kick-off.

2. We followed the crowd; all clad in red and all heading in the same direction.

3. Tickets checked, we entered the ground with a few minutes to spare.

4. It was a last minute decision to attend the match.

5. Nonetheless, we got there in good time and managed to park not far from the ground.

The sentences below were written about the astronaut Tim Peake. Show your understanding by answering the questions that follow.

1. In 2015 Tim lifted off in the Soyuz rocket to begin his Principia mission.

2. Peake served for 18 years in the British Army.

3. After that he was selected to be an astronaut and joined the European Space Agency.

4. Part of his job was to train people to fly Apache helicopters.

5. He completed extensive training before being selected for a mission to the International Space Station.

> **Stretch**
>
> Now try to find a piece of text that you could divide into five sentences. Consider whether it would make sense or how it would change the meaning if you were to put it back together in a different order.

   a. Which sentence should come second in the text? Write the number of the sentence below.

   ----

   b. Which sentence should come fifth in the text? Write the number of the sentence below.

Progress check

When you have received feedback from your teacher, complete the progress check below. Tick the box which you think best indicates your progress.

Skill being tested	I am working to achieve this skill	I have achieved this skill in places	I'm confident I've achieved this skill
Locating information in a text			
Practising the types of skills multiple-choice questions could test			
Understanding what a question requires			
Integrating evidence sensibly to support an answer			
Analysing evidence choices carefully and in detail			
Synthesizing details from more than one text			
Writing in more detail where the question requires it			
Critically evaluating a text			
Practising editing questions at word, sentence and text level			

Unit 2: Section B Writing

Summary of Unit 2: Section B Writing

Unit 2: Whole paper
• 40% of total marks for GCSE English Language
• Assessment length: 2 hours
• Section A Reading
• Section B Writing
Section B
• Half of the available marks for the paper (20% of total grade)
• Time required: 1 hour
• One proofreading task
• One writing task to be selected from a choice of two (could be description, narration or exposition)
• Half of the marks for the writing section (20 marks on B2) will be awarded for communication and organization (meaning, purpose, reader awareness and structure)
• Half of the marks for the writing section (5 marks on B1 and 15 marks on B2) will be awarded for writing accurately (language, grammar, punctuation and spelling)

Section B of Unit 2 will test your ability to write one piece of extended writing from a choice of two. The types of writing will be description, narration, or exposition. Where appropriate, this may require you to draw upon the reading materials used in Section A. Possible types of writing include biographies, memoirs, travel writing, food writing, diaries, stories and personal essays.

Section B will also include one proofreading task focusing on your awareness of accuracy in writing. You will be expected to proofread and correct a short text and this will be worth 2.5% of the qualification (5 marks).

Assessment Objectives

Section B Writing of the Unit 2 exam will test your abilities in the following assessment objectives (AOs):

- Write to communicate clearly and effectively, using and adapting register and forms and selecting vocabulary and style appropriate to the task in ways that engage the reader.
- Proofread and use linguistic, grammatical, structural and presentational features in their own writing to achieve particular effects, to engage and influence the reader and to support overall coherence.
- Use a range of sentence structures and paragraphs appropriately for clarity, purpose and effect, with accurate grammar, punctuation and spelling.

Activity 1

Based on what you have read, answer the following questions:

1. What percentage of your total marks come from the writing section of Unit 2?

   _____

2. Which two things are you assessed for on each writing task?

   _____

   _____

   _____

3. What do you know about the proofreading task that will be included in the writing section?

   _____

   _____

   _____

4. What types of skill are you assessed for in the communication and organization element?

   _____

   _____

   _____

5. How long should you spend on the writing section of the Unit 2 exam?

   _____

1 Writing: narration

Learning focus:

- To develop awareness of this type of writing
- To practise skills and techniques that will be needed

When you write using narration you will present the development of events from a personal point of view. This might take the form of a report, news story or personal account. You will need to use your own experiences (or experiences that you know about) to write in conjunction with the theme of Section A.

You will be given the time and space to plan your work in the exam and you should make use of this. Planning your work will ensure that you know what you are being asked to do because it will give you the chance to review your ideas. It will also help you to decide the direction your writing will take so that you can organize it effectively.

Activity 1

The following are tasks which might be set for a narration question. Complete the table with three more tasks that you think could be set for this part of the exam.

Write an account of a time when you had to look after an animal.
Write a report on the success of the school play for your school newspaper.
Write an account of a time when you enjoyed a school trip.
Write a report on an event run by your sports club for your local newspaper.
Write an account of a family celebration.

Think about how you will plan your work. You need a system that works for you and enables you to get your ideas down as quickly and sensibly as possible. For example, you might use a spider diagram, a table or a list of bullet points. Make sure that whatever system you choose helps you to organize your writing.

Activity 2

Using the following title, copy and complete the plan below:

> Write an account of a time when you enjoyed a school trip.

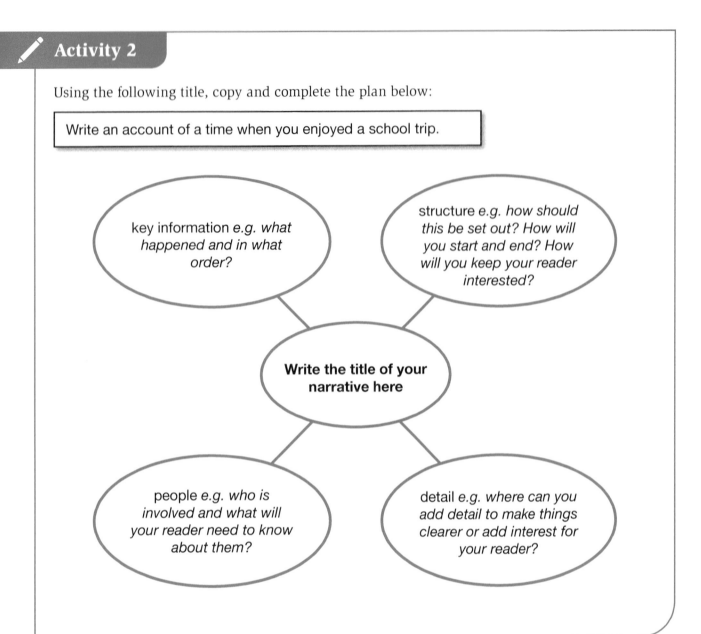

Now that you have planned a piece of writing you are going to practise some of the skills needed to write narratively. First consider writing an effective opening.

The following openings all respond to the title:

> Write an account of a time when you enjoyed a school trip.

Sample answer 1

On task

My most enjoyable school trip was when we went to an outdoor activities centre for a week. We were allowed a week out of school time to go and we had a great time. There were so many things to do that we didn't have the chance to be bored.

Closed statements – don't allow for candidate to elaborate

Moves on too soon

Examiner comment

Although this is on task it lacks the detail that would engage the reader. Rather than developing his/her ideas the writer is tempted to release too much information too soon and this shuts down ways in which the writing could develop.

Sample answer 2

Tone clearly positive – immediately links with enjoyment aspect of task

Gives specific information

The incredible residential week spent at Adventures Wales was my most enjoyable school trip ever. We were a group of around fifty students from Year 8 and Year 9, accompanied by five teachers. We set off on a bright June morning for Porthcawl in South Wales, where we were to spend a week taking part in exciting outdoor activities and intensive team building skills.

Pacing it well – begins at the beginning

Examiner comment

This answer sets the scene and the tone well and the reader is given initial information that will be developed. This candidate releases necessary information but does not try to tell too much too soon.

Activity 3

Using your plan from page 45, write your own opening paragraph. Try to engage the reader with initial detail but don't be tempted to give too much away too soon.

Activity 4

Now complete this piece of writing about a school trip you enjoyed.

Think about the following:

- Keep the task in mind – you are writing about things you enjoyed during the school trip.
- Refer to your plan – keep the end direction of this piece firmly in your mind.
- Be aware of using paragraphs effectively – a new paragraph is needed for changes in time, place, topic or person.

15 marks out of the 35 available for this task come from writing accurately. That means that your use of language, grammar, punctuation and spelling are worth almost as many marks as making your writing interesting and purposeful.

Activity 5

Look at the following paragraph, taken from a candidate's exam paper:

> We was ment to travel to Cardiff for a day at the museem. The bus came and all of our
>
> clas got on. Some of the lads shuvved there way to the back of the bus and refusd to move
>
> until Sir got on and said they wuld have to stay behind if they didn't. We were setting off
>
> and someone realises that they have left there bag in the classroom. We stopped while they
>
> went to fech it.

There are **ten** basic errors here. Some of them will have been caused by writing at speed during an exam. Use a coloured pen to correct the mistakes.

Sometimes while re-reading work we realize that we could have expressed things slightly differently. Look at the improvements made below:

Some of the lads shoved their way to the back of the bus and refused to move until Sir got on and said they would have to stay behind if they didn't.

Some of the lads shoved their way to the back of the bus. They refused to move until one of the teachers got involved. Mr Brunskill very quietly suggested some additional revision could be found for them at school if they weren't going to behave appropriately. Peace was quickly restored.

Activity 6

Only by writing regularly and practising some of these skills will they become automatic. Check your writing on page 47 and amend any errors. When you have done this choose one paragraph to make improvements to. Rewrite the final version below.

----

2 Proofreading

Learning focus:

- To revise and build on proofreading skills
- To consider some common errors

Proofreading your own writing will provide you with good practice for the proofreading element of the exam paper. Remember that errors could be in spelling, punctuation and/or grammar. Many candidates look for the spelling errors and neglect other mistakes. You will only get the marks in this section if you correctly *identify* and make clear the *correct* version of any error.

Activity 1

Pupils have been asked to design a permission slip to go out to parents. One student came up with the following. Can you identify and correct **five** errors?

My son/daghter _____ has my

permision to attend the school trip to the National Sceince

Museum. I understand that the class will be travel by coach and

that he/she needs to be at school no later than 7.15am on 21st

January. I can confirm that he/she will be collected from the coach

on it's return at 6:30pm.

Signed: _____ (parent/

guardian)

Homophones

Homophones are words that sound the same but have different meanings and/or spellings. For example, the words 'knew' and 'new' are homophones. Some homophones are more common than others and being able to recognize and avoid making mistakes with these will help you in both your own writing and when it comes to proofreading.

Activity 2

Ten examples of common homophones are written below. Write a sentence for each one that uses the word in the correct way. The first one has been done as an example.

Homophone	Example
there, their, they're	I was over there, near the entrance to the train station, when the incident happened.
affect, effect	
our, are	
weather, whether	
led, lead	
which, witch	
principle, principal	
to, two, too	
hear, here	
your, you're	

Activity 3

Read through your own work and find examples of three homophone types that you have made mistakes with. Write them out below and then find the definition of each word in a dictionary and add it.

Homophone	Definition

Activity 4

Complete the following sentences by deleting the incorrect homophone in each:

1. The chair of the bored/board of directors gave an extremely long speech, throughout which I was extremely bored/board.

2. We took the shortest route/root possible in order to return to school and route/root out the troublemakers.

3. The building sight/site was a disgraceful sight/site to all neighbours who had to look upon it.

4. Although she was no longer aloud/allowed in the building, she did not let this stop her speaking her thoughts aloud/allowed to all those gathered in the entrance.

5. He was exactly right/write in his decision to right/write a letter to the headteacher detailing his concerns.

Activity 5

Identifying the incorrect use of a homophone is one of the skills you may be tested on in proofreading activities. Identify and correct any incorrect words in the sentences below:

1. Only last weak the teacher had corrected these spellings on the bored.

2. She herd that the team was ready to go onto the pitch but when she got their they were nowhere to be scene.

3. He was aware that he should prey for his grandmother and tolled his brother to do the same.

4. There was a sail in the store and she was determined to purchase the pear of shoes she had been admiring all winter.

5. "Oh deer," said the coach when she realised the hall roof was leaking. "Now we'll have to practice on the field."

3 Writing: description

Learning focus:

- To develop awareness of requirements for description writing
- To practise skills and techniques for description writing

Description is writing about what something is like in order to help the reader form impressions. It may well be based on reality but the writer will be aiming to interest and possibly influence the personal feelings of the reader. Although you may read some descriptive texts that are non-continuous, you are most likely to be asked to write a piece of descriptive continuous text. This could take a number of different forms; some examples include a travelogue, a diary or an article.

As with all parts of the exam, it is important that you know what you are being asked to do. The sample question below has been annotated to show you the key words and how to interpret the question:

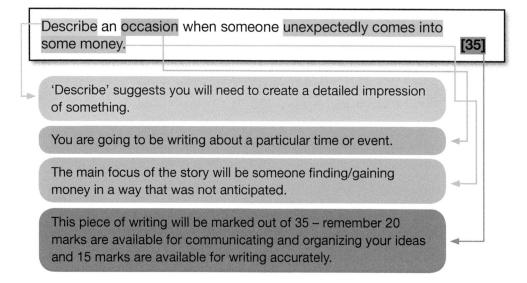

Describe an occasion when someone unexpectedly comes into some money. [35]

'Describe' suggests you will need to create a detailed impression of something.

You are going to be writing about a particular time or event.

The main focus of the story will be someone finding/gaining money in a way that was not anticipated.

This piece of writing will be marked out of 35 – remember 20 marks are available for communicating and organizing your ideas and 15 marks are available for writing accurately.

Below is an extract from the story *Millions* by Frank Cottrell Boyce. This story is written about two brothers who have an unexpected windfall.

I tried to say a prayer, but all I could think of to say was, 'In the name of the Father and of the Son and of the Holy Spirit, Amen. My Mum is Dead. Amen.'

Even that little prayer took me about five minutes to say because my teeth kept chattering. God must have heard me, though, because he answered it. And you know what. […] He gave me something.

Just as I finished the prayer a train went past. A huge gust of oily air […] I looked out. The train had no windows. It was just a huge block of night on wheels, screaming past the holly bushes.

As I watched, a little scrap of darkness seemed to get free of the big darkness and come rolling through the air towards me. […]

I went over and touched it. It was a bag. It had come apart along the zip and its insides were spilling out. And its insides were money. It wasn't a vision or a visitation as such. I suppose you could call it a sign. A big loud sign. It was money. Banknotes. Piles and piles of them. Thousands and thousands of pounds. Millions, even.

✏ Activity 1

In this extract the writer gives a detailed account of the arrival of the windfall. He does not state what events take place but adds details that will interest and engage the reader.

A straightforward statement of what takes place appears in the table below. Complete the middle column of the table by copying out the words from the text that match these statements. The first one is done as an example.

What happened	In the text	What does the writer do?
The prayer took a while to say because he was cold.	'Even that little prayer took me about five minutes to say because my teeth kept chattering'	Make us feel sympathy towards the boy. He shows us he is cold by mentioning his teeth 'chattering' which is more effective than telling us.
The train went past quickly.		

Activity 1 continued

It was a freight train.		
It was difficult to see the train.		
Something fell out of the train.		
The bag was open.		
There was a lot of money.		

Activity 2

Complete the third column of the table to explain what you think the writer does to make his writing more interesting than the basic statement of what happened.

Activity 3

You are going to write an answer to the following sample question.

Describe an occasion when someone unexpectedly comes into some money.   **[35]**

First think about what your unexpected windfall may be.

Write a short paragraph outlining ideas about the moment that your windfall arrives.

Activity 4

Look again at this question.

> Describe an occasion when someone unexpectedly comes into some money.　　[35]

Use the space below to plan the content of your writing.

You have an idea of what will take place in your account and have some detail about how the windfall arrives. Now think carefully about how you will start this piece and attract the attention of your reader.

Tips

- Starting to write is often the hardest part. The following ideas may help.
- Use one of the following opening lines to get you started. You can always alter it when you get going.
  - The day began in the most ordinary way…
  - She/he had always maintained that money was not everything, and so it would prove.
  - Looking back, I would do things so very differently.
- You could choose to begin with the windfall arrival and then go back to the start of the action (some care with tenses and careful signposting to your reader would be needed, though).

Activity 5

Write the first two or three paragraphs of your piece.

Revisiting your writing and seeing where detail can be enhanced is essential preparation for the exam.

The following paragraph has been improved to add appropriate detail to appeal to a reader.

> Greater emphasis could be given to the length of time spent playing and how it has previously felt hopeless.

> This point could be made more specifically – in what way?

The woman didn't look happy as she handed the ticket back to Blake.

"You've won," she confirmed.

"I've won?" Blake questioned. "I've really won?"

Blake could not believe it. She had won the lottery after all these years of playing it. She danced up and down on the spot in delight. Her topaz eyes shone with joy and happiness. Wow. She was rich.

> The character's thoughts could be conveyed with more immediacy.

> More specific detail could convey the excitement more clearly.

> Unnecessary vocab that detracts – the eye colour adds nothing.

Student answer

The woman wore a fake smile as she returned my ticket.

"You've won," she managed to confirm.

"I've won?" Blake questioned, in a state of some shock. "I've really won?"

Unbelievable. After all these years of seemingly pouring money down the drain on ticket after ticket, week after week, she'd finally won? Her legs took over in an impromptu jig as tears of happiness poured from her eyes. Wow. What a day! She was rich.

✎ Activity 6

Edit a paragraph or section of your writing from page 57, thinking particularly about how your writing might engage the reader. When you are happy with it rewrite the improved version here.

----

4 Sentencing

Learning focus:

- To revise the importance of accurate punctuation
- To practise writing accurate and well-controlled sentences

To score highly in an exam you must strive to make your writing as accurate as possible. If you know where your weaknesses are you will find it easier to avoid them.

In creative writing, it is important to vary your use of sentence structure to add interest to your writing. This includes using sentences of different lengths and types and sometimes using different kinds of sentence opening.

Sentence control is demonstrated through your use of punctuation, specifically, full stops. You should also understand the basic rules for using commas, capital letters, question marks, exclamation marks and for punctuating speech. One of the most common errors that examiners see is from candidates who neglect the basics and do not make sure they use full stops and capital letters accurately. This can significantly affect meaning and the coherence of your writing.

Activity 1

Rewrite the student answer below using complete sentences. Think about the punctuation and where capital letters are necessary.

Student answer

One day, our group went to the beach to have a day out in the hot, weather; it was a brilliant day and we all really enjoyed ourselves! the sun was shining and there was not a cloud in the sky so we knew it was going to be fun, my favourite part was when we had all been surfing in the sea and came back up to the rocks to have a campfire and barbecue. Rosie got her guitar out and played a song she had written herself; it was awesome!!! she should definitely go on X Factor.

Activity 2

Now correctly copy out the following section by choosing one of the punctuation choices on offer:

Student answer

The sea was stunning that day [. ,] showcasing deep sky blue pools that were occasionally spot lit with streaks of glittering turquoise [, !] it was a photographer's dream [. :] of course [, -] she did not notice any of this [? .] she was far too distracted by her young charges [. ,] two sun-tinged and lightly freckled boys [- ,] twins by the look of them [. ,] were charging towards the rock pools [. ,] their mum [. ,] who seemed both happy and a little flustered [, :] was close behind them.

Tip

Sometimes you need to know what follows each decision so read the whole extract with a pencil in hand before doing the rewrite.

_____

_____

_____

_____

_____

_____

_____

_____

Activity 3

Write the opening paragraph for a task entitled 'Memories of time spent by the sea'. This could be either a narrative recount of events or a description of an occasion. Think about the following advice:

- Prioritize the use of full stops and capital letters.
- Vary the length and type of your sentences.
- Try to avoid beginning every sentence in a similar way.

_____

_____

_____

_____

_____

_____

_____

5 Writing: exposition

Learning focus:

- To revise concept of expository writing
- To practise skills and techniques for use in expository writing

Expository writing provides an explanation of ideas from a personal viewpoint. It attempts to explain something in a way that helps the reader to understand what they are reading. Some examples of expository writing are essays which attempt to interpret or explain something, diagrams which help the reader understand concepts and books which aid learning such as textbooks and reference books.

To demonstrate expository writing in an exam you may be asked to write an essay giving your own personal views about a topic.

Personal views are not always presented in an obvious way. It is not necessary to signal every personal opinion with the words 'I think' or 'I feel', although you may wish to use these occasionally. In expository writing you should present your ideas from a **subjective** point of view but make the opinions and ideas that are presented the focus of your essay.

> **Key term**
>
> **Subjective:** based on or influenced by personal feelings, tastes or opinions

✏ Activity 1

Below are three titles that could have been set for this question.

1. Underline the key words in each question in order to establish the purpose of the essay.

2. Complete the ideas box for each question to show what you would write about if asked this question. Make sure you have at least three or four different ideas for each.

Essay title	Ideas
Write an essay explaining why money is important to teenagers.	• • • •
"It is really important that kids spend as much time travelling and learning as possible from a young age." (Sir Richard Branson) Write an essay to explain the extent to which you agree with this view.	• • • •
Write an essay in which you explore the impact that sport and exercise have had on your life.	• • • •

Activity 2

1. Expository writing has a formal tone. Complete the following sentence to show what you think this means:

    Formal writing is _____

    _____

2. Put a cross next to any of the following that you think you should avoid to ensure you are using a formal tone:

    Abbreviations (such as e.g. and etc.)   ☐

    A variety of phrases and sentence types   ☐

    Slang and colloquial language   ☐

    Varied vocabulary   ☐

    Contractions (can't, won't, shouldn't)   ☐

3. Rewrite the following sentences in a more formal way:

    Student answer

    I'm a teenager and money is dead important to me. I can't imagine life without money. My mates wouldn't be seen dead with me if I wore stuff that didn't have the right labels on it. That sort of thing costs and I for one don't mind paying for it. I need money to make sure my image etc. is sorted.

    _____

    _____

    _____

    _____

    _____

    _____

    _____

    _____

    _____

    _____

    _____

    _____

Tip

You may need to rephrase or reorder some of these sentences as well as change the vocabulary.

Now you are going to plan a piece of exposition writing. The structure of your writing is very important – the way you organize your ideas can make all the difference to whether a reader understands them or not.

✏️ **Activity 3**

Complete the following template:

Essay title: Write an essay explaining why money is important to teenagers.

Introduction:

Note down your aims/expected outcomes for this essay. An explanation of whether money is important to teenagers or not. How will you engage your reader's attention from the start? You could use a personal anecdote or a relevant fact to do this. You may wish to engage with your reader through questions or humour.

Point 1

Write down your most important reason why money is/isn't important to teenagers. In note form list any evidence/key points you don't want to miss in relation to this point.

Point 2

Write down your second point in relation to why money is/isn't important to teenagers. In note form list any evidence/key points you don't want to miss in relation to this point.

Point 3

Write down your third point in relation to why money is/isn't important to teenagers. In note form list any evidence/key points you don't want to miss in relation to this point.

Point 4

Are there additional points/evidence that you want to mention more briefly? Note them down here so that you can add them in if there is time.

Conclusion

A final summary in relation to the title. What conclusion do you expect to arrive at after making all of the points above? Your final statement should aim to keep your reader thinking about this topic, without simply repeating your points from above.

Activity 4

Review the plan you have just written. Think carefully about whether your points are ordered in the most sensible and effective way. Try to change at least one thing in order to make things clearer or to ensure that they link together more effectively.

In Activity 6 you are going to write your answer to the question. However, before you do this, think about the way that you will structure and organize your writing. It is important that writing is fluent and points link clearly and sensibly to one another. To prepare for this, look at the activity below.

Activity 5

Read the following extract from an article published in *The New York Times*.

In the last decade, Apple has become one of the mightiest, richest and most successful companies in the world, in part by mastering global manufacturing. Apple and its high-technology peers – as well as dozens of other American industries – have achieved a pace of innovation nearly unmatched in modern history.

However, the workers assembling iPhones, iPads and other devices often labour in harsh conditions, according to employees inside those plants, worker advocates and documents published by companies themselves. Problems are as varied as onerous work environments and serious – sometimes deadly – safety problems.

Employees work excessive overtime, in some cases seven days a week, and live in crowded dorms. Some say they stand so long that their legs swell until they can hardly walk. Under-age workers have helped build Apple's products, and the company's suppliers have improperly disposed of hazardous waste and falsified records, according to company reports and advocacy groups that, within China, are often considered reliable, independent monitors.

Activity 5   continued

More troubling, the groups say, is some suppliers' disregard for workers' health. Two years ago, 137 workers at an Apple supplier in eastern China were injured after they were ordered to use a poisonous chemical to clean iPhone screens. Within seven months last year, two explosions at iPad factories, including in Chengdu, killed four people and injured 77. Before those blasts, Apple had been alerted to hazardous conditions inside the Chengdu plant, according to a Chinese group that published that warning.

*peer – a person of the same age, status, or ability as another specified person
*advocates – a person who puts a case on someone else's behalf
*onerous – something involving a great deal of effort, trouble, or difficulty

Annotate this extract with the following comments. Spaces have been provided for you to do this.

The writer clearly dates the rise of Apple.

A negative or contrasting point is clearly signalled.

The writer makes Apple's success clear.

The sentence opening indicates that there is more negative information to follow.

The writer expands on the points made in the previous paragraph.

Activity 6

Using the notes that you have made and remembering what you have learned about organization and structure, write your answer to the following question:

Write an essay explaining why money is important to teenagers.

Now you are going to look back over your writing and think about where improvements could be made. To achieve high marks for communicating and organizing your ideas, the following can all add impact when used appropriately:

Effective writing with techniques that engage the reader.	This could be achieved in a variety of ways: For example: • rhetorical questions • figurative language • humour • hyperbole • techniques for emphasis – lists, exclamation, etc. • use of facts/evidence.
Clearly expressed, well-judged content.	This means content needs to be: • task focused • appropriate • interesting • presented in a way that does not confuse.
Detailed development of ideas.	This means you must have expanded your ideas – don't just state a point. For example: 'Teenagers need money in order to show they are responsible' could be developed into 'Money is necessary for a teenager to develop responsibility for himself or herself. If we need to budget and make decisions about what we need to spend our money on, then we will be building crucial life skills in a very practical way.'
Purposeful shape and structure to writing.	This means your paragraphs must follow logically and add a sense of purpose and development to your work. Remember that structure and shape are also assessed within paragraphs. Check that one sentence logically follows the next and so on.

Activity 7

Look back at your work and see if you have addressed the points in the table on page 67. Select one paragraph to rewrite and improve in the space below.

Progress check

When you have received feedback from your teacher, complete the progress check below. Tick the box which you think best indicates your progress.

Skill being tested	I am working to achieve this skill	I have achieved this skill in places	I'm confident I've achieved this skill
Planning a piece of writing			
Confident awareness of how a piece of writing is to end			
Practising the addition of detail to a piece of writing			
Proofreading own writing			
Recognizing homophones			
Using punctuation accurately to control writing			
Sequencing writing in a logical way			
Revisiting writing in order to improve it			

Unit 3: Section A Reading

Unit 3: Section A Reading

Unit 3: Whole paper
• 40% of total marks for GCSE English Language
• Assessment length: 2 hours
• Section A Reading
• Section B Writing

Section A
• Half of the available marks for the paper (20% of total grade)
• Time required: 1 hour
• Several texts to read
• At least one persuasion and one argumentation text
• Texts will be continuous and non-continuous
• There will be a range of structured questions with different mark tariffs

Section A of Unit 3 will test your ability to read at least one persuasion text and one argumentation text linked by a common theme. You will be assessed through a range of structured questions. The varied text and question types will require you to demonstrate different reading approaches and skills in answering. There will be both short-response (for example, multiple-choice questions, short answers, sequencing tests) and extended-response questions (for example, comprehension, analysis of text, explanation).

Assessment Objectives

Section A Reading of the Unit 3 exam will test your abilities in the following assessment objectives (AOs):

- Use inference and deduction skills to retrieve and analyse information.
- Synthesize and summarize information.
- Interpret themes, meaning, ideas and information.
- Edit texts and compare and evaluate usefulness, relevance and presentation of content.
- Refer to evidence within texts, distinguishing between statements that are supported by evidence and those that are not.
- Evaluate and reflect on the way in which texts may be interpreted differently according to the perspective of the reader.
- Understand and recognize the purpose and reliability of texts.

Activity 1

Based on what you have read answer the following questions:

1. How many of your total marks come from the reading section of Unit 3?

   _____

2. What types of text will you face in this section of this exam?

   _____

   _____

   _____

3. How long should you spend on the reading section of this exam?

   _____

4. How long will the Unit 3 exam last in total?

   _____

1 Interpreting information from different sources

Learning focus:

- To explore different text types
- To locate information in a range of different text types

In the exam you will be asked to consider a range of continuous and non-continuous texts. For this activity you will be focusing on non-continuous texts. You will need to use your reading skills to understand these texts and to extract the information required to answer the questions.

Activity 1

Graphs

A graph is a diagram that represents a system of connecting information (usually between two sets of numbers). There will be information along two axes at a right angle to each other. Answer the following questions about the graph below:

1. When did the survey take place?

   _____

2. Which group of people used mobile phones most frequently while driving?

   _____

3. What percentage of people in the 60 and over category used their phone while driving?

   _____

4. What was the total percentage of people in the 30–59 age group who used their phones while driving?

   _____

Use of handheld mobile phones by age of driver, England and Scotland

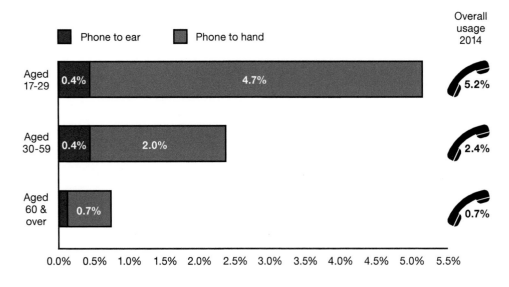

✏ Activity 2

Commenting on pictures and tables

BAD DRIVING PENALTIES	
Offence	Maximum penalty
Manslaughter	Life
Death by dangerous driving	14 years
Dangrous driving (incl. use of mobile phone or sat-nav)	Two years
Careless driving	£2,500 fine
Using a hand-held mobile while driving	Three points/£60 fine

Pictures can convey a lot of information. You might want to comment on a picture when completing a 'how' question. You could be asked to make a link between the picture and the text.

1. How does the combination of the image and the table effectively demonstrate bad driving and its penalties?

    List any reasons that you can think of.

    *   _____
    *   _____
    *   _____
    *   _____

2. What is the maximum punishment for someone who uses their phone while driving?

    _____

Activity 3

Reading texts with a clear purpose

This text aims to persuade the reader to complete a specific action (that is, to buy a new mobile phone). Understanding why a text has been produced can help you to understand the content better.

1. Write down the simile used by the writer. Explain what this simile means and its effect on the reader.

   _____

   _____

   _____

   _____

2. Why do you think the writer includes a range of icons behind the image of the phone?

   _____

   _____

3. The writer gives some key details in a smaller white font. What message are they trying to put across about this phone?

   _____

   _____

Activity 4

Linking information across a text

Some texts may use a key or a range of different symbols to present information. The image below gives a range of details about worldwide mobile phone use.

1. Which of the named countries has the most mobile phones?

   _____

2. Which of the named countries has the least mobile phones?

   _____

3. The image suggests that some countries have more than 100% of people owning a mobile phone. What do you think this actually means?

   _____

4. A huge proportion of Africa is coloured green. What does this suggest?

   _____

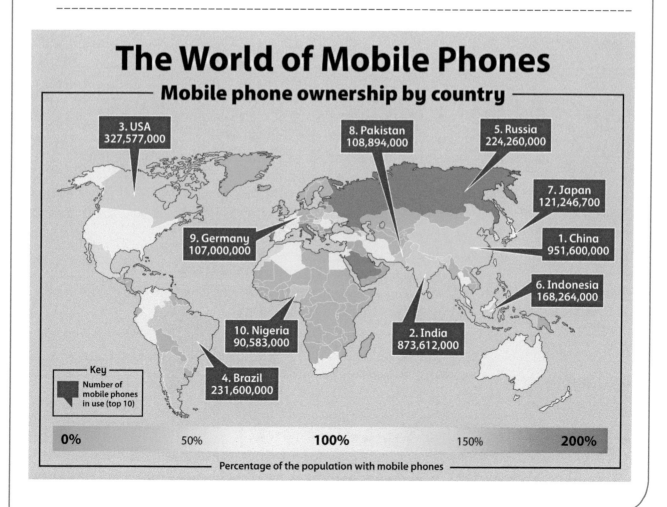

The World of Mobile Phones
Mobile phone ownership by country

3. USA
327,577,000

8. Pakistan
108,894,000

5. Russia
224,260,000

7. Japan
121,246,700

9. Germany
107,000,000

1. China
951,600,000

6. Indonesia
168,264,000

10. Nigeria
90,583,000

2. India
873,612,000

Key
Number of mobile phones in use (top 10)

4. Brazil
231,600,000

0%　　50%　　100%　　150%　　200%

Percentage of the population with mobile phones

2 Deducing meaning

Learning focus:

- To revisit the skills required when deducing meaning
- To practise exploring the meaning of words and phrases
- To use skills for reading in context to help understanding

The following text contains some complicated language. You will need to use a range of reading skills to help you deduce the meaning of some of the language.

The lost art of handwriting

Do you remember learning to write? I loved writing so much during my childhood years that I constantly reinvented my script, dotting my 'i's with little hearts, or switching between a round 'a' and one with a little arm above the circle. I filled endless diary pages, sent mail to pen pals, even invented secret symbols to ensure notes passed in the classroom were indecipherable by enemy eyes. But no longer. Today I barely lift a pen or a pencil to scribble a shopping list (my iPhone notepad function is far easier), and as a result, when I do have cause to abandon a keyboard in favour of a more old-fashioned tool, the result is at best sloppy, and more often than not illegible.

Technology seems to have ruined our collective handwriting ability. The digital age, with its typing and its texting, has left us unable to jot down the simplest of notes with anything like penmanship. A third of us can't even read our own writing, let alone anyone else's.

There are some very good reasons why we should brush up on our writing skills. Many application forms are still completed the old-fashioned way, as are the majority of school assignments, both of which allow us to be judged – in part at least – by the way we form letters on the page.

Then there are the more subjective arguments from those who consider writing to be an art form, a historical tradition, a means of expression. And this I fully support. At university I took a minor in Japanese and, for four years, studied the detailed strokes that make up the three types of script used in that language – hiragana, katakana and kanji. I saw the beauty of lettering afresh, and dedicated myself to becoming an artist of sorts.

But then I went on to become a journalist and spent countless hours learning yet another script – shorthand. Designed for speed rather than style, it helped my interview technique but not my legibility. Added to the growing importance of texting and tweeting and messaging and emailing in my life, it was the last nail in the coffin for the beautiful handwriting of my childhood…

Activity 1

Read the text carefully then answer the questions that follow.

1. What does the writer mean by 'indecipherable'?

   a. Closely folded notes ☐

   b. Not able to be read or understood ☐

   c. Able to be read and understood by others ☐

   d. Writing that is legible ☐

✏ **Activity 1   continued**

2. What does the writer mean by 'more old-fashioned tool'? Use the text to explain the reason for your answer.

_____

_____

_____

_____

_____

_____

3. The writer mentions her 'penmanship'. What does this mean?

    a. A technology tool that allows you to write via a computer   ☐

    b. Pens that have been specifically designed for men   ☐

    c. People who use a pen for a living   ☐

    d. The art or skill of writing by hand   ☐

4. The writer mentions 'subjective arguments'. What does this phrase mean?

_____

_____

_____

_____

_____

5. What does the writer mean by 'afresh'?

_____

_____

_____

_____

_____

_____

Tip

It might help if you briefly refer to the rest of the paragraph when explaining the meaning.

3 The purpose of a text

Learning objectives:

* To revise purpose of text definitions
* To work out the purpose of a range of different texts

In the exam, you will be asked to read through a text and then you will have to work out its **purpose**. For this exam, the purpose of a text will be defined as either:

* public
* personal
* occupational
* educational.

It is essential that all students are familiar with these purposes and their definitions. This question in the exam will usually be tested in a multiple-choice format.

Activity 1

Remind yourself of the different purposes of a text and match each type to its definition below.

Personal	Linked to action – linked to achieving a goal
Public	Texts that instruct – reading to acquire information
Occupational	Relating to public issues/activities and concerns
Educational	Written for personal interest and often read during leisure time

In the exam, the question or questions relating to purpose of text will take on a similar format to the one below:

Tick the box that best describes the purpose of this text:

a) Personal use ☐

b) Public use ☐

c) Occupational use ☐

d) Educational use ☐

✏ Activity 2

Look at the following texts. Write down the purpose of each text and a short sentence to explain your reasoning.

Purpose:

_____

Reason:

_____

_____

How To Protect Your Computer Against Viruses

On the computer, turn on the firewall

Keep the computer operating system up to date

Use updated antivirus software on the computer

Purpose:

_____

Reason:

_____

_____

✏ Activity 2 continued

Purpose:

_____

Reason:

_____

_____

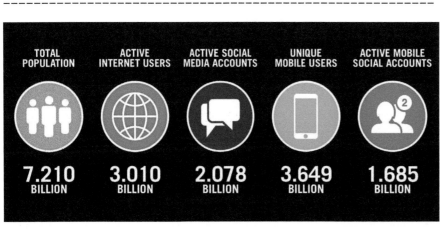

Purpose:

_____

Reason:

_____

_____

Activity 3

The table below asks you to give three examples of each type of text that you may encounter when working on purpose of text. Complete the table. A couple of examples have been included to guide you.

Purpose	Example 1	Example 2	Example 3
Personal	Article on fashion in a magazine		
Public			
Occupational		Advert inviting people to apply for a part-time job	
Educational			Instructions on how to build your new computer

Activity 4

Throughout this book there are a range of different texts. Look at a range of different texts that you may have at home (newspapers, cereal boxes, magazines, etc.). Choose five different texts and see if you can work out their purpose.

Tip

When trying to work out the purpose of a text, it's important to get a sense of the whole article. Read the text carefully; do not just scan one or two words or details.

Activity 5

Now write your two top tips for working out the purpose of a text.

1. _____
   _____

2. _____
   _____

4 Sequencing information

Learning objectives:

- To understand what is meant by 'sequencing information'
- To develop sequencing skills

Key terms

Sequence: arrange in a particular order

Logical: correctly reasoned

Chronological: the order in which things occurred

When you are asked to **sequence** information you have to put a series of instructions into a **logical** order. This type of activity requires you to think in a **chronological** way.

Activity 1

Think about a simple activity that you do every day that requires you to complete actions in a certain order; for example, the steps you take in order to make your breakfast. Write down four simple steps that you follow and number them 1–4.

Activity 2

The following instructions should be completed in order. Number each step of the following text from 1–4 to put it into a chronological sequence. For each step, give a reason which says why you believe it should appear in that order.

☐ Using your method, gather information and results to help you complete your study.

- - - - - - - - - - - - - - - - - -

- - - - - - - - - - - - - - - - - -

☐ Select a research method. What is the best way to answer your question?

- - - - - - - - - - - - - - - - - - -

- - - - - - - - - - - - - - - - - -

If you are completing a research project you need to complete the following steps

☐ Identify the focus of your research. Ask the question, what are you going to research?

- - - - - - - - - - - - - - - - - -

- - - - - - - - - - - - - - - - - -

☐ Analyse the information you have gathered and present your results.

- - - - - - - - - - - - - - - - - -

- - - - - - - - - - - - - - - - - -

Activity 3

Occasionally words will be used to help you work out a sequence; for example, *next, finally, after this*.

Think of four other words like this and write them down in the space below.

Tip

Sometimes words from one step in a sequence will appear in another step. You can use this to help you work out the correct order. For example: '... analyse the information you have gathered ...'. You know this step will come after the one where you have to gather information.

Activity 4

Now sequence the following two texts using the tips above to help you.

1.

☐ When you have located the instruction manual, carefully read the instruction 'Before you start...'

☐ Now you can start your build. You must follow each step of the instruction manual, in order.

☐ In your instruction manual you will see a list of tools that are required for the job. Make sure you have these before starting your build.

☐ Open the package and check all items have been included, including the instruction manual.

2.

☐ Make a list of features or applications that are essential to you.

☐ Research which phones have the features that you require. Make a list of these phones.

Steps to consider when purchasing a new mobile phone

☐ Work out a budget for your new phone. You can't make any decisions until you know what you can afford.

☐ Visit a mobile phone retailer and ask to see/try the different phones on your list. This will allow you to get a feel for each phone and hopefully make the right choice.

5 Summarizing text

Learning focus:

* To revise summary skills
* To practise using summary skills in exam-style tasks

In the exam you will be asked to produce a **summary** of a text or to summarize information across more than one text.

To produce an effective summary keep the following points in mind:
* Read the text closely and highlight the main ideas.
* Look at **topic sentences** which may summarize information within a paragraph.
* Look at your highlighted words/phrases. Can you link any of these?
* Put your highlighted words/phrases into your own words.
* Never add any additional ideas or opinions.
* Keep your comments brief or use bullet points.

Key terms

Summary: a brief document or statement that gives the main points of something. It is a shortened version of a longer text which is written up in the reader's own words. Producing a summary tests your understanding of what you have read

Topic sentence: often the first sentence in a paragraph, it tells the reader what the paragraph is about, and is followed by other sentences which give more detail

Activity 1

1. Think about a recent film or television programme you have watched. Can you summarize what happened? Write your summary in the space below. Do not use any extra space.

   _____
   _____
   _____
   _____
   _____

2. Go back through the summary of your film. Are there any areas where you can further reduce the words you have used?

   _____
   _____
   _____
   _____

✎ Activity 2

Look at the text below. The subheadings have been removed. Read each section carefully and summarize the information from within each paragraph to produce a brief subheading.

Parents: do your teens text too much?

If it seems like your teen's fingers are glued to their cell phone, you might have a problem. While tapping away might seem innocent, there are risks associated with too much texting. On average, teens send or receive 3,339 texts a month, and that can do damage to more than just your monthly bill. Find out how too much texting can be a serious teen issue.

It's a chicken and egg scenario – excessive texting is linked to risky behaviour. A 2010 study found that too much texting was a predictor of risky behaviour like substance abuse or smoking. In fact, teens who "hypertext" – send more than 120 text messages per day – were 43 percent more likely to be binge drinkers and 55 percent more likely to get in a physical fight.

When you send your teen to school in the morning, you probably hope that they make the most of the opportunity to learn. Unfortunately, with a cell phone attached to their hand, texting could prove to be too much of a distraction. Even if your teen isn't sending the messages, they could be receiving them, breaking their concentration in school, and causing a distraction. Even if your teen's school forbids texting in class, teens often find secretive ways of sending messages.

Texting while driving is seriously dangerous behaviour. 11 percent of drivers who were in a car accident admitted to be sending or receiving a text message when the accident occurred. Texting while driving takes your teen's eyes and concentration off the road, so they are less alert and slower to react. It's simply unacceptable behaviour, and it's especially a problem for new drivers who should give their full attention to the road – not to a text message.

While texting isn't exactly an extreme sport, it doesn't mean your teen can text night and day without any physical effects. Too much texting can actually lead to tendinitis. Similar to typing on a computer or completing the same motion over and over, tendinitis can cause pain, aching and throbbing in the wrist and in the thumb as a result of your teen's incessant texting.

Tip

A summary, like a heading, only gives key details so it should be brief.

Activity 3

One way to develop your summary skills is to work through a passage and to remove any words that are not required. The remaining words will produce the details required for your summary.

1. Work through the passage below deleting any words that you do not think are necessary. Make sure the information continues to make sense.

How mobiles have created a generation without manners: Three in four people think phones, laptops and social media have made us ruder

For anyone who has had to wait for service while a shop assistant finished surfing the net on a smartphone, it will not come as a shock. The latest handsets and other mobile devices may be helping a new generation to stay safer and better connected... but it's making them ruder. About three in four people now believe manners have been wrecked by phones, laptops, tablets and social media such as Facebook and Twitter.

A report warned that company executives are now watching to check if their young employees are becoming over-dependent on their smartphones in the office. Some are 'so over-reliant on computers and spellchecks that they don't even know how to write a letter any more'. According to yesterday's report, 'the introduction of advanced mobile technology and superfast connectivity to businesses has boosted the Treasury by billions of pounds and will continue to do so for decades to come. However, the pitfalls of over-reliance on technology are being revealed.' A survey carried out by One Poll among 1,000 people found that 77 per cent think social skills now are worse than they were 20 years ago, and 72 per cent think mobiles have encouraged rudeness.

The Etiquette Consultancy also conducted a study among a group of 58 senior executives which found that well over half looked for social skills rather than academic achievement in candidates for promotion. They believed that a major problem among young employees was 'constant use of mobile phones and social media in the office'. A majority felt the written skills of young employees were 'appalling'. The report cited 'a rift between virtual and real world personalities', saying that only 15 per cent of the people in its poll would feel confident walking into a room where they didn't know anybody, while 62 per cent would be confident about creating a profile on a social networking site. One in four are uncomfortable about meeting a new colleague face-to-face, and nearly half say they are nervous when they have to stand up in a meeting and give a formal presentation.

✎ Activity 3   continued

2. Now that you have cut the text down to the essential words and phrases, try to summarize
    the article in the space below. Try to limit your information to 50 words.

✎ Activity 4

A summary requires quick thinking and the ability to be decisive. You can revise your
summary skills by trying the following:

*   Summarize a book you have read.
*   Summarize the key things you did at school this week.
*   Summarize your actions on a specific day.

Choose one of the areas above and allow yourself 2–3 minutes to produce a brief summary.

----

6 How is an argument presented?

Learning focus:

- To consider whether texts provide **fact**, evidence, **opinion** or bias
- To revise the language associated with the reliability of a text

To demonstrate your understanding of an argument, you could be asked to consider not just the evidence presented but the way in which the writer has constructed their argument and whether the information is trustworthy or not.

Key terms

Fact: a thing that is known to have happened and/or to be true

Opinion: a personal view or judgement formed about something, not necessarily based on fact or knowledge

Activity 1

In this activity you need to decide whether each statement is a fact or an opinion by ticking the correct box.

	Fact	Opinion
There are four seasons each year.		
The government is responsible for flooding as they do not dredge rivers.		
English is one of the three core subjects at school.		
English is the most important subject at school.		
London is the capital of England.		
Cardiff is a much friendlier city than London.		
Water is far more precious than gold or diamonds.		
Water is made up of hydrogen and oxygen.		
People who use their mobile phones while in the bathroom are disgusting.		

Activity 2

Look at the statements below. Work out if each one is describing a factual statement or an opinion and tick the correct box.

	Factual statement	Opinion
The evidence is believable.		
The writer has used phrases like 'think' and 'seem'.		
The writer has used comparative adjectives like 'better' or 'tastier'.		
The writer has used subjective adjectives like 'pretty' or 'boring'.		
The information can be proved by experts or statistics.		

Activity 3

Now that we have a clear distinction between fact and opinion, we can look more closely at some of the other terms associated with the reliability of a text. See if you can match each term to the correct definition.

Evidence — Not influenced by personal feelings or opinions

Objective — A strong feeling in favour of or against one group of people, or one side in an argument, often not based on fair judgement

Bias — A view based on or influenced by personal feelings, tastes or opinions

Subjective — The facts, signs or objects that make you believe that something is true

Activity 4

Use two different colours to highlight the following text.
Colour 1: factual or evidence-based information
Colour 2: opinion, subjective information or bias

Mobile phones and driving

Police data confirms that using a mobile phone while driving is the biggest health risk posed by mobile phones. It can increase your chances of having an accident by 33%, and it's illegal to use a handheld mobile phone while driving or riding a motorbike. It is also thoughtless and ignorant.

People who do use their mobile devices while driving ought to have to retake their driving test to make them a better driver. Statistics show that it is not just young people who drive dangerously by using mobile phones. 65% of people over the age of 40 are guilty of this crime. There are punishments for those who phone and drive and from February 27 2007, the penalty for using a handheld mobile phone while driving increased to £100 and three penalty points added to the drivers' licence. This fine is still not enough for such a serious crime.

Activity 5

Read the text on page 90 and then respond to the question that follows. While you are reading, ask yourself:

* How reliable is the information?
* What facts can I refer to?
* What evidence can I use in my answer?
* How much of the information is subjective?

Activity 5 continued

How damaging are mobile phones?

With insufficient research, the answer to this question is that we just don't know. There have been so many studies on mobile phones and an awful lot of rumours but there's nothing concrete to suggest that using a mobile phone will have serious health effects. The technology at our fingertips is so new that scientists themselves don't fully understand effects of things such as radiation. However, the research does suggest that we need to be cautious and reduce the risk of exposure.

Parents need to carefully monitor their children's phone use. Because they have thinner skin, they absorb more radiation than adults and with less dense bones and a higher water content in their tissues, they are more susceptible to any side effects. Too much screen time has some other damaging effects such as loss of social interaction, face to face communication and cognitive development*. It's definitely best to limit your child's exposure to mobile phones as we just don't know how much damage we are causing.

What can you do? Ear plugs are a great idea for phone users as they move the phone physically away from your body. It is advisable for people to put their phones into airplane mode to limit the radiation emitted and to carry them away from the body (for example, in a backpack).

It's not a question we can answer easily so limit your phone use until we have more concrete evidence and information about mobile devices.

Cognitive development – how thought processes are constructed from childhood through to adulthood, including remembering, problem solving and decision-making

Select five arguments from the text above to help you answer the following question.

Does the writer convince you that mobile phones are harmful?

_____

_____

_____

_____

_____

_____

_____

_____

_____

7 Answering a 'how' question

Learning focus:

- To revise how to approach a 'how' question
- To practise textual analysis skills

Closely linked to considering the reliability of information is considering how a writer has put together their text or argument to maximize its effect on a reader. A 'how does the writer…' question tests how well you have understood the text and also what the writer is hoping to achieve.

When answering a 'how' question:
- Read the question carefully to help you understand exactly what you are being asked to analyse.
- Find evidence to support your views and to help you answer the question.
- Consider any methods used by the writer to help them reinforce their message.
- Link your ideas back to the question.

✏ Activity 1

Using the tips above, annotate the two questions below to show that you understand what you are being asked to do:

> How does the writer persuade the reader that mobile phones are beneficial in modern-day life?

> 'Global warming is a threat.' How does the writer persuade you that this statement is true?

✎ Activity 2

Many students struggle to understand what to comment on when they are asked to look at the writer's techniques or methods. The trick here is to only comment on techniques if you have something worthwhile to say.

Consider this question:

> How does the head teacher persuade parents to join the school laptop scheme?

Below is a list of evidence that a student has selected from a text to help them answer this question. Use the evidence to complete the table below.

Evidence	Method used	Why would this persuade parents?
85% of students who join this scheme pass all of their GCSE exams…		
Our IT technicians will fix any problems and can offer 24-hour support.		
Which? magazine suggests these laptops are number one for quality, design and portability.		
Do you really want to deny your child the chance of success?		
If you sign up today, we will throw in a free laptop bag worth £45.00.		

Activity 3

Look at the sample response below. A student has written an answer to the question in the previous activity and has been told to redo it by their teacher.

1. Read through the answer and see if you can work out where they need to improve their work. Annotate the answer below.

Student answer

The head teacher tries hard to persuade parents to buy a laptop. They use a number of techniques. The first way they persuade is by using a rhetorical question. This type of question does not need an answer and gets the parents to think. The head teacher uses repetition to put across their message so it is reinforced. The head teacher uses an expert opinion from Which? as this would definitely make people want to invest in a laptop. The sentences used are short so there is not a lot to read and this would make parents happier to listen. Facts and statistics are also used to make sure we believe what the head teacher is saying.

2. Write down three ways this student could improve their answer:

- _____

  _____

- _____

  _____

- _____

  _____

Activity 4

Read the text below and answer the question that follows. Try not to spend more than 15 minutes answering the question.

Pupils 'losing marks in exams due to poor handwriting'

Students may be missing out on vital marks in GCSEs and A-levels because of a significant deterioration in handwriting skills. It was claimed that a decline in traditional handwriting skills was directly linked to an over-reliance on technology in classrooms.

Previous research has suggested that children who struggle to write fluently devote more brain capacity to getting words onto a page during tests – interfering with their ability to generate ideas, select vocabulary or plan work properly. The Government has pledged to improve standards, with handwriting playing a bigger part in the newly revamped National Curriculum. Schools are now required to hold lessons in handwriting for five- to seven-year-olds, with pupils being expected to hold pencils properly and form letters correctly and confidently.

Commenting on the study, Tony Sewell, an education writer and former teacher, said: "Clarity of handwriting isn't just important in ensuring exam questions are answered in a clear manner, but is a critical part of the learning process. The fluid motion of writing and rewriting notes helps to instill the data in the mind more efficiently than the process of typing, making it an effective revision tool which aids information recall."

According to figures, 61 per cent of teachers believe there has been "deterioration in the quality of handwriting among students in the last five years". Almost two-thirds – 64 per cent – admit that illegible writing "has prevented them from awarding the full marks a student deserved", while 35 per cent said they had found emoticons in exam answers. 82 per cent of teachers believe students are losing other traditional skills such as mental arithmetic "due to over-reliance on technology".

Margaret White, a handwriting expert, said: "Lack of practice – when you aren't using a pen and paper to take notes on a regular basis – means it's easy to slip into bad writing habits, such as gripping the pen too tightly or applying too much pressure on the paper. This can make writing uncomfortable, not to mention inefficient, so it's unsurprising nearly half of students tell us they suffer from aching hands after lengthy exams. 15 per cent even report getting blisters."

Students themselves admitted to shunning handwriting. 89 per cent of those responding to the poll said they now revised using laptops and computers, while more than half deemed the "traditional method of note-taking with a pen and paper outdated".

Activity 4 continued

> How does the writer persuade us that technology is having a negative effect in schools and exams? **[10]**

Activity 5

1. Go back through your answer and in three different colours underline the following:
   - the evidence used to support your answer
   - any reference to the writer's method
   - any clear references to the question.

Do you have a balance of colours? How many different areas did you manage to cover in 15 minutes?

2. Write down two tips that will help you the next time you complete a 'how' question.

----

8 How to compare texts

Learning focus:

- To revise what is meant by a comparison
- To explore how to compare information presented in texts

You will be asked to compare two or more texts in at least one of your English exams. A comparison question is usually one of the last questions you will be asked to complete as you will have already read and answered questions about the texts. When comparing texts you will be given a specific focus to ensure your answer does not become too vague.

Activity 1

1. Write down a definition of the words 'compare' and 'comparison'. You may use a dictionary to help you.

   Compare

   _____

   _____

   _____

   Comparison

   _____

   _____

   _____

2. Make a list of words you might use when comparing one thing to another. Two have been given for you.

   Although

   But

   _____

   _____

   _____

   _____

   _____

   _____

The next two texts give views about mobile phone use.

Text A

Our children will suffer for our mobile phone addiction

Two little boys had just been to a football match. Bubbling with enthusiasm for what they had just seen, the pair of them – about eight and 10-years-old – jumped from foot to foot, chattering with each other and trying to engage their mother in conversation too.

But their mum had absolutely no interest. As the boys skipped and shouted and tugged at her arm she continued to poke, poke, poke at her mobile phone, fully engaged in whatever text, email, internet snippet or game had popped up on the screen. This scene unfolded in front of me last week at Waterloo Station and I found it heartbreaking. A couple of wonderful children, keen, full of life, eager to communicate with their mother but she's not interested.

Millions of people are linked to each other remotely by phone and, as a result, completely detached from the people and events around them. John Lennon's adage that "life is something that happens when we're busy doing something else" has never seemed so apposite*.

In the US a movement is beginning to build against the technology that is nibbling away at family relationships: the unholy alliance of Facebook, Twitter and instant messaging that is destroying social interaction and turning us into a planet full of screen-watchers. We need a similar movement in Britain. My question, always, is why is the mobile phone such an object of fascination to so many people? If it is simply because it links us 24 hours a day to our friends and family, what on earth are people finding to say to each other minute by minute, hour by hour?

apposite – something that is suitable or appropriate to the discussion

Text B

Why we can't live without our mobile phones

Our attachment to our mobile phones is only going to worsen as the manufacturers continue to up their game, writes Emma Barnett.

The rise of 'nomophobia' – the fear of being without your mobile phone – is completely understandable.

As smartphones increasingly become the norm for most of the nation, I am shocked that only 66 per cent of those recently polled on this issue, said they were suffering from this 21st century syndrome.

I recently left my phone at home on a work day and I genuinely felt panicked without it. My phone is now my email device, camera, games console, Twitter dashboard and social network controller – all rolled into one.

Despite how pathetic the reliance will seem to some, we are now at the tipping point. More than 50 per cent of the nation now claim to suffer from this new phobia and understandably so.

The camera industry, games companies and even the PC providers are all competing with this one device – which has rolled several gadgets into one – and is doing it better every year.

Admittedly, it's a pleasure on a non-work day to forget your phone. It's important to disconnect and have some down time. In fact at the start of this year, we wrote about the need for the 'digital diet'.

However, the increase of our reliance on our phones has happened so rapidly, that I can remember a time, only three years ago, when I wouldn't check my work emails during the evening.

Now that thought seems incomprehensible. Whether or not it's bad for us, our addiction to our phones is here to stay and 'nomophobia' will understandably continue to rise, as the mobile manufacturers continue to up their game.

Activity 2

1. After reading the two texts on page 97, compare the following:
    *   the writers' views of mobile phone use
    *   the reasons the writers give for their views.

    Complete the table below to organize your points and evidence, and to ensure you get a clear grasp of the writers' views.

Text A		Text B	
View of mobile phone use	Reason for view	View of mobile phone use	Reason for view

2. When you have completed the table go back through each column and see if you can organize the information into positive or negative views.

3. Now look back through your points. Can you see any views or reasons that can be linked? If so, draw a line to link them.

4. Look again at the points you have drawn out. Are any of them distinctly different? If so, write a brief note to remind you of what the differences are.

Activity 3

Now you are ready to write your comparison of Text A and Text B. Some students like to begin with a very brief overview to give an overall insight into the writers' views. See if you can use your summary skills to help you to produce an overview.

You might like to consider a sentence similar to the one below to get you started.

> Text A is concerned about the effect of... whereas Text B focuses on the reliance... In Text A...

Activity 3 continued

Now start your answer here and continue onto separate paper.

_____
_____
_____
_____
_____
_____
_____
_____
_____
_____
_____
_____
_____

Tips

- Make it clear which text is being referred to.
- Support claims with evidence.
- Base your answer on the text, not on personal viewpoints.
- Timing is key – comparison will often be a later question but with higher marks available.
- Make sure both/all texts receive consideration.
- Read the question carefully – what is the focus of the comparison?

Progress check

When you have received feedback from your teacher, complete the progress check below. Tick the box which you think best indicates your progress.

Skill being tested	I am working to achieve this skill	I have achieved this skill in places	I'm confident I've achieved this skill
Locating key details in a text			
Working out the meaning of words and phrases in a text			
Understanding the purpose of a text			
Sequencing information			
How to produce a summary			
Understanding how an argument is presented			
How does the writer…			
The ability to compare texts			

Unit 3: Section B Writing

Summary of Unit 3: Section B Writing

Unit 3: Whole paper
• 40% of total marks for GCSE English Language
• Assessment length: 2 hours
• Section A Reading
• Section B Writing
Section B
• Half of the available marks for the paper (20% of total grade)
• Time required: 1 hour
• Two compulsory tasks to complete
• One argumentation task
• One persuasion task

Section B of Unit 3 will test your ability to read and understand two writing tasks and produce a piece of writing in response to each task. Both tasks will have a thematic link to the materials you have read during Section A of the exam. You may use information gained from the reading section to help you generate some ideas for your writing. It is vital that you add your own ideas, though; do not purely copy from the reading resources.

Assessment Objectives

Section B Writing of the Unit 3 exam will test your abilities in the following assessment objectives (AOs):

- Write to communicate clearly and effectively, using and adapting register and forms, selecting vocabulary and style appropriate to task and purpose in ways that engage the reader.
- Proofread and use linguistic, grammatical, structural and presentational features in your own writing to achieve particular effects, to engage and influence the reader and to support overall coherence.
- Use a range of sentence structures and paragraphs appropriately for clarity, purpose and effect, with accurate grammar, punctuation and spelling.

Activity 1

Based on what you have read answer the following questions:

1. How many of your total marks come from the writing section of Unit 3?

   _____

2. What types of task will you face when writing in this exam?

   _____

   _____

   _____

3. How long should you spend on the writing section of this exam?

   _____

4. How long will the Unit 3 exam last in total?

   _____

1 Argumentation writing

Learning focus:

- To revise what is meant by argumentation writing
- To consider how to approach different argumentation tasks

Argumentation is writing which presents a view of a topic. When tackling this type of writing you will need to decide what your view is on a given issue or topic and then present that view. You might find yourself considering a range of different viewpoints on a given topic.

Argumentation writing can include tasks such as a letter to an editor, a report or an article about a specific topic, idea or event.

Activity 1

Below is a sample exam question. Read the question carefully and plan how you might approach this task.

> A number of students have complained about the lack of clubs at your school. Write a report for your school council in which you argue for new clubs to be introduced.

Report for school council on new clubs

What did you include? Tick any boxes that apply to your plan.

- ☐ Suggestions for new clubs.
- ☐ Reasons for suggesting new clubs.
- ☐ Ideas on how to make the introduction of new clubs easier.
- ☐ Detailed suggestions (who will run it, when, where, etc.).
- ☐ A range of reasons for new club suggestions.
- ☐ A summary.

Activity 2

When producing argumentation writing, it is important that you present a clear view on your given topic. To help you generate some ideas, answer the questions below.

1. Write down three topics that you feel strongly about.

    ----

2. If you could get rid of something in society, what would it be and why?

    ----

3. Think about the news topics you see, hear or read about. Are there any topics that make you feel either angry or sad? Why do you think you feel this way?

Activity 3

Look carefully at the picture below and respond to the task that follows.

Activity 3 continued

You are being asked to put together a piece of writing that gives your view on why we should support WaterAid, a charity that provides safe water and toilets to areas which need them. You can use the picture on page 103 to help you come up with some ideas.

Use the space below to plan what you would include in your writing.

Activity 3 continued

2 Preparing to write

Learning focus:

- To explore how to plan during the examination
- To experiment with different planning techniques

A good plan can help you to produce a clear and well-organized piece of writing. Many students struggle with what to include in a plan and how much time to spend on it.

Activity 1

Read the following planning suggestions and put them into a logical order by adding numbers in the boxes provided.

- Work out the audience, purpose and format for the writing. ☐
- Read the task carefully and work out what you are being asked to write. ☐
- Think about organizing your ideas into a beginning, middle and end. ☐
- Jot down your initial ideas – you could use a spider diagram or a list. ☐
- Read through your initial ideas and see if you can add any extra details/language to help you. ☐
- Number the points you have included to help you sequence your ideas. ☐

Activity 2

Using a spider diagram

Read the statement in the centre of the spider diagram and the questions on page 106 then complete the plan.

You have strong views about the statement and want to share these with your class.

'Many young people in our country are selfish, badly behaved and have poor manners. They only think of themselves.'

Activity 2 continued

Do you agree or disagree with the statement? Why?

Have you any experience of these areas?

What language will you use to convey a strong view?

Can you think of any examples to either agree or disagree with the statement?

Activity 3

List planning

Some people prefer to use a list of notes to help them to organize their ideas. This approach can help you to produce a well-organized piece of writing.

Read the task below.

> Wales has invested heavily in tourism over the last decade. Do you think more people should spend their holidays in Wales rather than travelling abroad?

Look at how one student listed their ideas:

- Yes – intro to agree with the statement.
- Give examples of holidays my family have taken in Wales.
- Give examples of some tourist destinations in Wales.
- Give examples of tourist attractions in Wales.
- Give negatives of travelling abroad.

Can you think of any other areas you might like to include? Complete your own more detailed plan on this topic in the space below.

Introduction – outline your main views on the topic (do you agree/disagree with the statement?)

Paragraph 1

✏ Activity 3   continued

Paragraph 2

Paragraph 3

Paragraph 4

Conclusion – summarize your ideas and give an overall view on the topic

----

Tips

- You are not awarded marks for your planning so do not spend too much time on it (5 minutes maximum), but careful planning will help you gain higher marks for your writing.
- There is no one correct way to plan – experiment with ways that suit you best.

3 Using reading material to help you

Learning focus:

- To consider what to include from the reading materials in your writing exam
- To explore techniques for including reading facts

In your Unit 3 exam, section A will be on a specific topic and the writing tasks will be loosely related to this topic. You do not have to use the reading sources to help you with your writing but it is fine to include some facts or details from section A.

✎ Activity 1

Read the sample task below and the text that follows.

> Your head teacher is considering banning mobile phones in school. You have decided to write a letter to your head teacher giving your views on the proposal.

The text below could have been used in the reading exam and could be used to help you. Highlight any areas in this text that you would use to help you complete the task above.

BUT WOULD IT WORK?

SUGGESTED EDUCATIONAL USES FOR PHONES IN CLASS
- Listening to foreign language podcast recordings
- Setting homework reminders
- Recording a teacher's poetry reading for revision

AND HOW PUPILS MIGHT BE MORE LIKELY TO USE THEM
- Texting friends
- Surfing the internet
- Taking pictures of a teacher
- Playing electronic games

Now write a brief plan for the task on separate paper.

Activity 2

Another way of including details is to quote the source material. Bill Bryson produced this article about a train journey to Llandudno. If you were asked to argue why an area of Wales is beautiful you could quote one or two phrases from this source.

1. Read through and highlight any phrases you might use.

    Then suddenly the caravan parks thinned, the landscape around Colwyn Bay took on a blush of beauty and grandeur, the train made a sharp jag north and minutes later we were in Llandudno.

    It is truly a fine and handsome place, built on a generously proportioned bay and lined along its broad front with a huddle of prim but gracious 19th-century hotels that reminded me in the fading light of a line-up of Victorian nannies.

2. Add a quote to the sample response to suggest why people should visit North Wales:

    North Wales is often overlooked as a holiday destination but those who do visit find themselves faced with spectacular rugged scenery, picturesque beaches and impressive historic buildings. Bill Bryson commented, "...

Activity 3

You have been asked to produce an article giving your views on handwriting. Using the article, 'The lost art of handwriting' on page 76, make a list of five ideas or quotes from the text that you can use in your article.

*   --
    ----
*   --
    ----
*   --
    ----
*   --
    ----
*   --

Tip

Do not copy large sections of the reading exam texts, as you will not be credited for copying. Quote or include helpful phrases and carefully selected details.

4 How to structure your writing

Learning focus:

- To revise how to structure a piece of writing
- To develop structure within a paragraph

Teachers often remind students to write in paragraphs and to consider a clear beginning, middle and end for their writing. How these things link together can have a huge impact on the quality of your writing.

Activity 1

1. Think about something you really enjoy doing in your spare time. Think about how you would summarize the activity by writing down one or two words to describe each stage of the activity (for example, meet friends, play football, cool down).

Beginning

Middle

End

----

2. Now add some finer details (for example, arguing about teams, comments on players and their positions, location). Think carefully about the logical sequence of the activity and adding enough detail so that anyone reading has a clear understanding of what you do.

Activity 2

Read the following task then look at the plan on page 111.

> Write a letter which argues why technology is beneficial for teenagers.

Activity 2 continued

- Conclusion – bring ideas together and give some personal overview/comments
- Socializing – teenagers communicate more, build more friendships, can be more organized
- Homework – easy to get online support, research is instant and up to date, busy parents not required
- Apps – quality apps can promote good health, the ability to monitor activity and check for problems
- Intro – give overview of benefits/main uses/types of technology
- Political and social awareness – instant news, aware of what is happening
- Skills – improved IT skills, improved literacy and numeracy, ability to check spellings instantly

The student has plenty of ideas but has not organized these logically. Organize the ideas by deciding the order you think makes most sense. Write your order in the space below.

The structure of each individual paragraph is important. If the paragraph can be linked to the previous one, then do so. Use topic sentences to organize your writing. Think about the order of the information within the paragraph.

Activity 3

Complete the following sentences to help you write a clear introductory paragraph about the benefits of technology on homework.

Topic sentence: Technology has enormous benefits for _____

The internet allows students to _____

It also makes it easy for us to _____

In addition to this students can _____

Critics may claim that we get distracted but _____

Without computers _____

Activity 4

Now choose another idea from Activity 2 (for example socializing). See if you can write a detailed paragraph using a topic sentence and five or six supporting sentences.

_____

_____

_____

_____

_____

_____

_____

_____

_____

_____

_____

_____

_____

_____

_____

_____

Tip

Think of structure as a human body. The skeleton is your plan but you need lots of other items to cover the bones (the details) and many of these will link together to produce a complete person (complete piece of writing).

5 Developing language

Learning focus:

- To consider how to use language to have an effect on a reader
- To improve use of language in sample writing tasks

The language you select to use in your writing can have an impact on the reader and on the effect of your writing. Choosing effective language is a skill. If language is repetitive and simple the writing may become quite dull, but if the language is overworked (too many big words used inappropriately) the writing can lose its effect and overall meaning.

Activity 1

Read the following question:

> Choose a charity that is important to you. Write an article explaining why others should support this charity.

Some candidates choose to think about effective words they could use while planning their work. Look at the plan below and write down some emotive words you could use when writing this article. Two have been added for you.

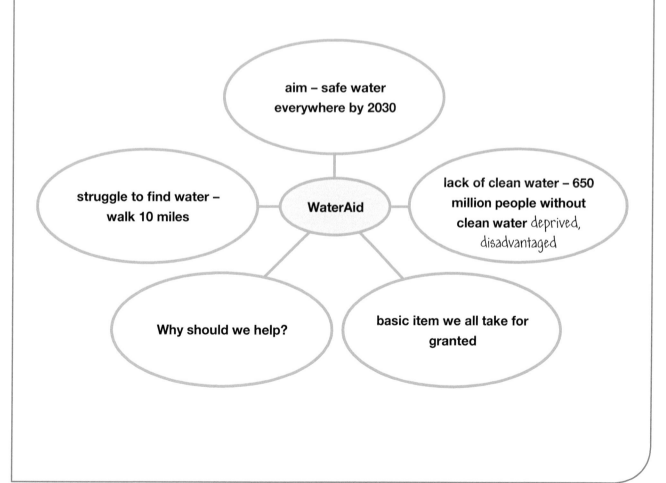

aim – safe water everywhere by 2030

struggle to find water – walk 10 miles

WaterAid

lack of clean water – 650 million people without clean water deprived, disadvantaged

Why should we help?

basic item we all take for granted

Activity 2

The writing below has been taken from a student's article. Fill in the spaces with your choice of appropriate words. You may use a thesaurus to help you to improve some of your vocabulary.

Doesn't everyone have the right to _____ water?
It _____ to me that 650 million people in our world do not have
_____ to this very basic necessity. We take fresh water for granted but
there are so many people in our world who would _____ if they could
drink fresh water every day. Don't you feel _____ when you realize that
just £1.00 could make a _____ difference?

Activity 3

You can practise varying the language you use by selecting a word and then writing down **synonyms** for that word. Try adding two or three alternatives for each of the common words below.

Big _____

Small _____

Sad _____

Bad _____

Good _____

Said _____

Boring _____

Key term

Synonym: a word that means the same thing or something very similar

Activity 4

Select a recent piece of your writing. Go back through your work and highlight any words that you feel you could change to improve your work. In pencil, write down alternative words you could use.

Tip

It is an excellent idea to go through your work and make your own personalized list of words that you have trouble spelling correctly. You can then focus on practising how to spell those words that you struggle to get right.

6 Persuasion writing

Learning focus:

- To revise what is meant by persuasion writing
- To consider how to approach different persuasion tasks

Persuasion is a type of writing which aims to convince a reader of the writer's viewpoint. Persuasive texts can include a speech to a given audience, a letter of protest or a review of a book or film.

Activity 1

1. Write down three situations when someone might try to persuade you to do something.

    - --
    - --
    - --

2. Write down three situations when you have persuaded someone else to do something.

    - --
    - --
    - --

Activity 2

1. The following text has been produced by a student to persuade their classmates to sign up for a school trip. Read through the text carefully and highlight any words or phrases that have been used to persuade others.

    I have to be honest, when I first heard about the school trip to climb Mount Snowdon I was less than excited... I mean, who wants to spend their weekend away from their family, home comforts and mobile phone?

    Then it struck me. We get to spend a whole weekend together having fun and getting away from the stresses of teenage life. Picture this: you're sitting with your favourite friends around a campfire toasting marshmallows. Does life get any better? You don't need to worry about your appearance for once and your phone won't beep every other second to tell you that 'Sam is feeling tired...' You won't have your parents nagging you to revise and complete more homework. Sound good yet?

    Not only will you spend a night under the stars (well, with a tent over you of course) but you get to enjoy plenty of fresh air and good old exercise. So what are you waiting for? This is going to be fun, fun, fun.

    Sign up today for a truly unmissable experience. What are you waiting for?

Activity 2 continued

2. The following table includes a list of some of the techniques that could be used to persuade a reader. Next to each technique write down an example from the text on page 115.

Technique	Example from the passage
Rhetorical question	
Repetition	
Imperative verb	
Specific details	
Direct appeal	
Appealing or emotive language	

Activity 3

In the text in Activity 2 a student tried to persuade their classmates to sign up for a camping trip. Re-read the passage. Thinking about the techniques and language used, try to write a similar text to persuade a classmate not to go on the camping trip.

1. Start by planning what you will write.

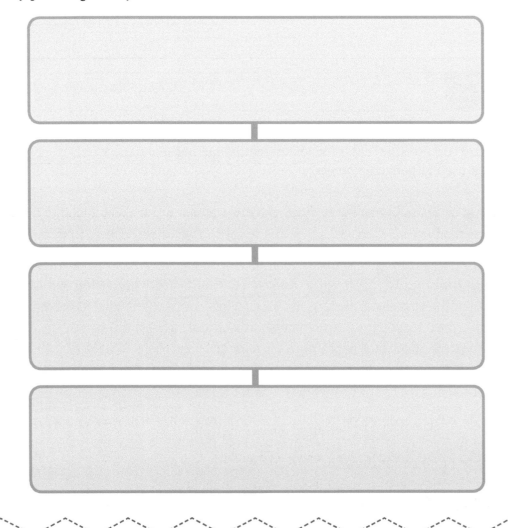

Activity 3   continued

2. Now write up your ideas. Think carefully about the techniques you want to use to ensure your classmates do not want to go on the trip.

Activity 4

Look at the writing you have just completed and tick any of the following statements that apply to your writing.

I planned my work carefully and thought about the sequence of my ideas.	☐
My writing had a clear title and I wrote in paragraphs.	☐
I included at least five different persuasive techniques.	☐
I varied the types of sentence I used in my writing to make it more interesting and persuasive.	☐

7 Developing detail

Learning focus:

- To explore what is meant by detail and development in writing
- To consider techniques to expand the level of detail in written work

The details that you include in your writing are particularly important. Many students produce writing that is brief or lacking in substance, which limits the number of marks that they are awarded. When writing you need to think carefully about the needs of your reader and ensure that you include sufficient details to engage them.

Activity 1

1. If you were asked to write an article to persuade people to study at your school or college, what would you include? Complete the plan below.

> **Introduction**

> **Paragraph 1**

> **Paragraph 2**

> **Paragraph 3**

> **Conclusion**

2. Now look again at each section of your plan. Add a few additional words to each section to help you add details.

Activity 2

The piece of writing below would receive low marks for content.

Why should you choose my school?

How? Why?

For example…

Introduction

School X is a very good school that gets good marks. The school is popular so many people want to come here. If you want to come to this school you will need to live in the area otherwise you don't stand a chance of getting in.

How do you know?

Which area? Where is it?

Doesn't make it sound interesting.

Lessons

We have all of the usual lessons at our school but there are a few others that are not so common. You can study law for GCSE as well as Italian and Japanese. The lessons are interesting and the teachers are all good. We have six IT classrooms so there's a strong chance that you'll use computers often too.

Expand on these.

How? Why?

1. Look at the teacher's comments. Can you see any other areas where you feel the student needs to develop their ideas?

2. Look back through the comments. Can you add a few ideas that would help this student to develop details in this piece?

3. Rewrite the passage making sure that you make the school sound appealing and that you persuade other students to want to study there.

Activity 3

Look back at the improved passage and complete the following in different colours.

1. Highlight any area where you have included specific details.

2. Highlight each use of varied punctuation.

3. Highlight any words or phrases that you feel are effective or add detail.

4. Highlight any words/phrases that you feel could be improved to have more of an effect.

8 Achieving the right tone

Learning focus:

- To revise what is meant by tone
- To explore a range of different tones that can be used in writing

Getting the right **tone** is important in your writing. If you choose a tone that is inappropriate – for example, too formal or informal – then your writing will not successfully answer the task that has been set and you will lose marks.

Activity 1

Look at the different types of tone in the table below. Try to think of an example of a situation in which you could use each tone type.

Tone	Situation
Formal	Job application
Factual	
Emotional	
Threatening	
Serious	
Friendly	
Persuasive	
Chatty	Email to a friend

Activity 2

Read the sample tasks below. Next to each task write down the audience, format, tone and your initial ideas.

1. Write a letter persuading the people in your local community to get involved in tidying the local park.

   Audience:

   Format:

   Tone:

Activity 2 continued

Initial ideas:

----

2. You feel that there are behaviour issues at your school. Write a report for your head teacher persuading them that there are problems and suggesting solutions.

    Audience:

    Format:

    Tone:

    Initial ideas:

    ----

3. Write a lively article for teenagers persuading them to try an extreme sport.

    Audience:

    Format:

    Tone:

    Initial ideas:

Activity 3

Tone is closely linked to the choice of language. The passage below is dull when it should be lively.

> Many people decide to do a parachute jump for a charity they want to raise money for. This is a good fundraising event as it is classed as an extreme activity.
>
> When you arrive at the parachute centre ready for your parachute jump you will feel a bit worried as well as a bit excited. This is normal. Just take a few deep breaths and make sure you are following all of the instructions. The instructors are good at what they do so they will have everything ready for your jump.

1. Can you rewrite the passage to make it sound exciting and lively?

   _____
   _____
   _____
   _____
   _____
   _____
   _____
   _____
   _____
   _____

2. Re-read your version of the passage. Highlight any language you have used that makes the passage exciting and upbeat.

3. Write down three words to describe the tone of the original passage.

   _____

4. Write down three words to describe the tone of the new passage.

   _____

5. If you were going to complete this piece of writing, make a list of the language you would use to describe the actual parachute jump.

   _____
   _____
   _____
   _____

9 Using your writing skills

Learning focus:

- To use the skills you have developed in this chapter to plan and write an argumentation task and a persuasion task

You have learned in this chapter that in your Unit 3 exam you will have one hour to complete two writing tasks. One piece of writing will be a persuasive task while the other will be an argumentation task. Remind yourself of the assessment objectives that are assessed in this section of the exam on page 101.

✏ Activity 1

Look at the criteria for the band you are working towards and write down three prompts for aspects that you feel you need to develop.

1. _____

   _____

   _____

2. _____

   _____

   _____

3. _____

   _____

   _____

In this lesson you will follow the steps outlined in this chapter to produce a piece of writing.

Re-read the article 'Parents: do your teens text too much?' on page 85 and look at the task below.

'Young people should not be given a mobile phone until they leave school at 16. Before 16, they are just too irresponsible to own one.'

You see the article above in a newspaper. You feel very strongly about the article and decide to write a letter in response. **[20]**

Activity 2

Use the space below to plan your work.

Activity 3

Before you start to write, think about the following:

* Who is the audience for your writing?

  _____

* Do you agree or disagree with the statement and why?

  _____

  _____

* What arguments will you put forward?

  _____

  _____

  _____

  _____

  _____

* How will you use the source material on page 85?

  _____

  _____

  _____

  _____

* What type of tone will you use?

  _____

* Make a list of words that will help you when you come to write out your answer.

  _____

  _____

  _____

  _____

  _____

  _____

  _____

  _____

  _____

  _____

  _____

Activity 3 continued

- Write your answer here

Activity 4

In this chapter you have been asked to consider the charity WaterAid. Now choose another charity that you feel needs support.

> Write the text for a leaflet about the charity in which you persuade others to donate their time and money to this good cause. **[20]**

Use the space below to plan your work.

Activity 5

Before you start to write, think about the following:

- Who is the audience for your writing?

- Which charity will you support and why?

- What techniques will you use to further encourage your audience?

- What type of tone will you use?

- Make a list of words that will help you when you come to write out your answer.

Activity 5 continued

- Start your answer here and continue on separate paper.

Progress check

When you have received feedback from your teacher, complete the progress check below. Tick the box which you think best indicates your progress.

Skill being tested	I am working to achieve this skill	I have achieved this skill in places	I'm confident I've achieved this skill
Planning writing			
Writing to persuade			
Writing to argue			
Structuring a piece of writing			
Using language effectively			
Developing detail in writing			
Using an appropriate tone			

Sample exam papers

Sample Unit 2

Reading and Writing: Description, Narration and Exposition

Section A Reading: 40 marks

Text A

A1 According to the text, what is a World Heritage Site? **[1]**

A2 Which organization decides on which sites are to become World Heritage Sites? **[1]**

Text B

A3 According to the table, which region has the third highest percentage of World Heritage Sites? **[1]**

A4 The additional information provided beneath the table refers to certain properties as 'trans-regional'. Select one definition from the list below which best describes 'trans-regional'. **[1]**

  (a) The same property has been rebuilt in all locations ☐

  (b) The property extends across several regions ☐

  (c) The property moves between regions ☐

  (d) The property is specific to one location ☐

A5 According to the graph, how many individual countries have 30 or more World Heritage Sites? **[1]**

Text C

A6 Tick the box that best describes the purpose of this text: **[1]**

  (a) Personal use ☐

  (b) Public use ☐

  (c) Occupational use ☐

  (d) Educational use ☐

A7 Use the text to summarize **three** of the aims of the Blaenavon World Heritage Centre. **[3]**

Text D

A 8 Which of the following are **not** attractions that can be visited at Blaenavon? **[1]**

(a) Big Pit National Coal Museum ☐

(b) Blaenavon Ironworks ☐

(c) World Heritage Centre ☐

(d) Heritage Railway ☐

(e) South Wales Route of Industrial Heritage ☐

Texts C and D

A 9 Synthesize the information presented about Blaenavon in these texts. **[8]**

Text E

A 10 The narrator mentions that he could choose between work in the furnaces or attending the 'Abergavenny Hiring Fair'. What type of work would he have been doing if he had chosen to go to the Hiring Fair? **[1]**

A 11 What impressions do you get about the life of a working child in these times? **[5]**

Text F

A 12 What does David Black mean when he describes Edinburgh as 'a magnet to visitors'? **[1]**

A 13 Explain why David Black thinks that being designated a World Heritage Site has been a disadvantage to Edinburgh. **[10]**

You must use evidence from the text to support your answer.

Editing (5 marks)

In this part of the paper you will be assessed for the quality of your understanding and editing skills.

1. Read the following sentence:

Now he had taken the chance to think things over, he knew that work difficulties were the cause of all of his problems. **[1]**

Which one of the following words could replace the word 'cause' without changing the meaning:?

(A) justification **(B)** grounds **(C)** answer **(D)** basis

2. Read the sentences below and then answer the questions that follow:

He paused momentarily in (1)_____ as the surf crashed around him. Sam had waited so long for the perfect conditions and now he was (2)_____ for the ride of his life.

(a) Circle the word below that best fits gap (1):

(A) fear   **(B)** anticipation   **(C)** reluctance   **(D)** sleep

(b) Circle the word below that best fits gap (2):

(A) having   **(B)** set   **(C)** teetering   **(D)** patient   **[2]**

3. Read the text below which consists of sentences in the wrong order and show your understanding by answering the questions that follow:

(1) 'It's twenty-five past three, they should have been out five minutes ago,' one agitated father complained.

(2) At last, the double doors opened and a stream of children began to emerge.

(3) The clouds darkened as a collection of parents began to group around the gates to the school.

(4) The rain grew heavier as more than one person could be seen to check their watch.

(5) Gradually, umbrellas were put up and waterproof pushchair covers attached.

(a) Which sentence should come **first** in the text? Write the number of the sentence below

---   **[1]**

(b) Which sentence should come **third** in the text? Write the number of the sentence below

---   **[1]**

Section B Writing: 40 marks

B1. *In this task you will be assessed for the quality of your **proofreading**.*

Read the text below taken from the website of a hotel.
Identify and correct 5 errors.

[5]

Great Eastern Hotel Pontypool

Great Eastern Hotel Pontypool is located in the centre of the town of Pontypool but has grate transport links to Cardiff and the Bay. Youll be close to the World Heritage site of Blaenavon, in addition to all of the tourist attraccions of the capital city. All of our rooms were en-suite and have tea and coffee making facilties.

Grade: 3 star

Type: hotel

Location: Pontypool

Telephone: 0745 234 567

Email: greateastern@totalhotels.co.uk

B2. *In this section you will be assessed for the quality of your **writing** skills.*

20 marks are awarded for communication and organization; 15 marks are awarded for writing accurately.

You should aim to write about 350–500 words.

Choose one of the following for your writing:

[35]

Either, **(a)** Write a report on any building or area that you think should be protected for future generations to enjoy and why.

Or, **(b)** Write a travelogue or diary entry to describe your visit to a place of historical significance.

Reading and Writing: Description, Narration and Exposition
Resource materials

Text A is a definition of a World Heritage Site from an online dictionary.

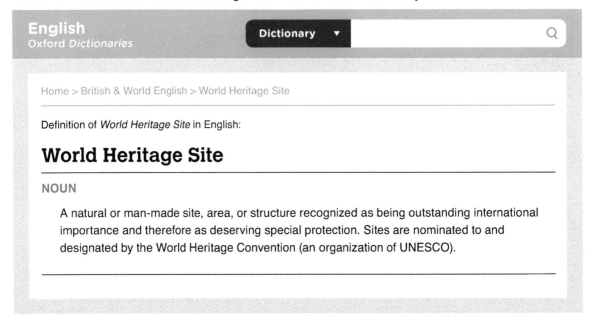

Text B provides information regarding the geographic location of World Heritage Sites.

				2016		
Regions	Cultural	Natural	Mixed	Total	%	States Parties with inscribed properties
Africa	48	37	5	90	9%	33
Arabic States	73	5	3	81	8%	18
Asia and the Pacific	172	62	12	246*	23%	36
Europe and North America	426	62	10	498*	47%	50
Latin America and the Caribbean	95	37	5	137*	13%	28
Total	814	203	35	1052	100%	165

*The property 'Uvs Nuur Basin' (Mongolia, Russian Federation) is a trans-regional property located in Europe and Asia and the Pacific region. It is counted here in the Asia and the Pacific region.

*Property 'The Architectural Work of Le Corbusier, an Outstanding Contribution to the Modern Movement' (Argentina, Belgium, France, Germany, India, Japan, Switzerland) is a trans-regional property located in Europe, Asia and the Pacific and Latin America and the Caribbean region. It is counted here in the Europe and North America region.

Text B continued

Territorial division

The following overview lists only countries with ten or more World Heritage Sites, updated through July 2016.

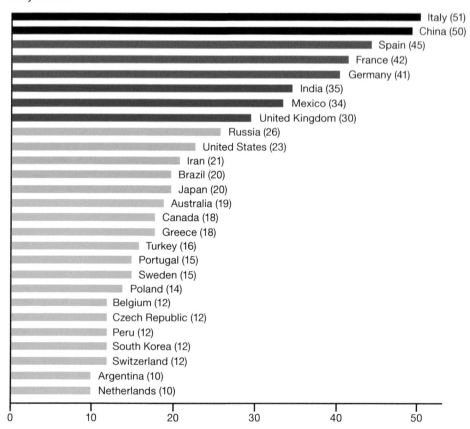

Italy (51)
China (50)
Spain (45)
France (42)
Germany (41)
India (35)
Mexico (34)
United Kingdom (30)
Russia (26)
United States (23)
Iran (21)
Brazil (20)
Japan (20)
Australia (19)
Canada (18)
Greece (18)
Turkey (16)
Portugal (15)
Sweden (15)
Poland (14)
Belgium (12)
Czech Republic (12)
Peru (12)
South Korea (12)
Switzerland (12)
Argentina (10)
Netherlands (10)

0   10   20   30   40   50

Text C is from the website of Torfaen County Borough.

Skip to Search | Skip to Content | Listen | A-Z of Services   Cymraeg

TORFAEN COUNTY BOROUGH   BWRDEISTREF SIROL TORFAEN   Stay Connected
Sign up for news and alerts

Home » Leisure Parks & Events » Tourism & Travel » Things to Do » Blaenavon World Heritage Centre and Library

Blaenavon World Heritage Centre and Library

Location: Blaenavon

Located in two beautifully restored former industrial schools from the early 19th Century, the Heritage Centre is the perfect place to being a visit to the Blaenavon World Heritage Site. The Centre features an interactive Victorian schoolroom, film and multi-media displays which not only provide visitors with a unique insight into the significance of Blaenavon's Industrial Landscape, but also introduces them to the area's many attractions. Make use of the Tourist Information Centre and visit the gift shop, café and library.

Open Tuesday-Sunday, 10am-5pm and Bank Holiday Mondays; last admission 30 minutes before closing. Closed 25 December-1 January inclusive.

Admission: Free

Text D is from Blaenavon's own website.

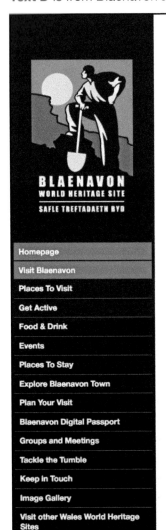

Homepage

Visit Blaenavon

Places To Visit

Get Active

Food & Drink

Events

Places To Stay

Explore Blaenavon Town

Plan Your Visit

Blaenavon Digital Passport

Groups and Meetings

Tackle the Tumble

Keep in Touch

Image Gallery

Visit other Wales World Heritage Sites

☑ Sign up to our eNewsletter   Search this site   Search

Visit Blaenavon
Real people, unique stories, great adventures

VISIT BLAENAVON

Located at the gateway to the South Wales Valleys, partly within the Brecon Beacons National Park, the Blaenavon Industrial Landscape is a testament to the human endeavour of miners and ironworkers of the past.

Set in 33 square kilometres, the attractions, events, activities and landscape make a perfect destination for a day out. The main attractions such as **Big Pit National Coal Museum**, **Blaenavon Ironworks**, the **World Heritage Centre** and **Blaenavon Heritage Railway** are all just a few minutes' drive or walk from each other. Indeed, there are so many brilliant attractions that you need to spend more than a day here to enjoy everything – so plan a weekend if you can!

In 2000, UNESCO inscribed the Blaenavon Industrial Landscape as a World Heritage Site, for the part the area played as the world's major producer of iron and coal in the 19th Century. Today you can see remains of all of the necessary elements needed for the iron and coal industry, including a coal mine, furnaces, quarries, railway systems, ironworkers' cottages, churches, chapels, a school and a workmen's hall. All set in a landscape that is favoured by walkers, cyclists and mountain bikers. Enjoy your visit – whenever you come!

And, once you've fully explored Blaenavon World Heritage Site why not discover more about Wales, the first industrial nation, by following the South Wales Route of Industrial Heritage, part of a Europe wide route.

Text E is an extract taken from the novel *Rape of the Fair Country* by Alexander Cordell.

On my eighth birthday my father put my name on the books of the ironmaster and took me to work at the Garndyrus furnaces. It was either the furnaces or the Abergavenny Hiring Fair, and I chose the furnaces, for some of the farmers were devils with the stick. Starting work at eight years old was late to begin a career, for some of the children in town began work at seven, or earlier. Take Sara Roberts – she was about my age but she had been chipping the rock from the iron vein since she was five, and Ieun Mathers lost one foot under a tram at five and the other when he was six. Still, there was no comparison between my family and the likes of these. The Roberts sat a long way behind us in Chapel for their father was a plain limestone digger, work that could be done by the foreigners, and he took home a bare three pounds a six weeks. My father, on the other hand, was a forge expert lent to Garndyrus by Mr Crawshay Bailey of Nantyglo, and was paid twice as much. So the fourpence a week Sara took home made a deal of difference.

Text F is adapted from an article in *The Guardian* newspaper.

Why Edinburgh should be stripped of its Unesco world heritage status

Recent planning decisions are trashing the historic centre of the Scottish capital – and its Unesco world heritage status isn't worth the paper it's printed on

David Black

It's easy to see why Edinburgh, one of Britain's most beautiful cities, is a magnet to visitors from across the world. It is also a place that instils pride and affection in those, like myself, who are native to it. Yet, this is a city that consistently undervalues its best asset: its historic centre.

It seems remarkable that Edinburgh's unique architectural character should be at risk. It was the largely unspoilt juxtaposition* of Old and New Towns that persuaded Unesco to grant it world heritage status in 1995. Yet the destruction during the 20 years since poses an interesting question: is Unesco world heritage status worth the paper it's printed on?

Edinburgh's role as a quality European destination underpins its economy, bringing in an annual £1.6bn to its coffers and its architectural heritage plays a huge role in this. That is why I am submitting a report to […] Unesco […] to persuade them to overturn the city's world heritage status.

Edinburgh's glory – and its marketability – is based on a stock of buildings that include Europe's oldest inhabited Royal Palace, Holyrood, and a medieval castle perched on a looming rock. […] Its sheer beauty can take the breath away. Look west from Calton Hill into a sunset of liquid gold and it's easy to see why Benjamin Franklin's business partner […] told him it was the finest view anywhere. Try the morning prospect from Arthur's Seat towards the Royal High School for some inkling of the scene that inspired Mendelssohn to write his Scottish symphony. Make the most of it, though. Hall's view south will now include the anodyne* "New Waverley" precinct. […]

Why do the powers-that-be want to trash this treasure? By "powers that be" I don't simply refer to the local council, which seems minded to sanction developer mediocrity on an alarming scale. There's also the Scottish government, which has declared an intention to offload the most architecturally significant public building in Scotland – Robert Adam's General Register House. […] Or how about the National Trust for Scotland, which decamped from its neoclassical headquarters in Charlotte Square to another out-of-town […] settlement.

Unesco has been known to take punitive action. For building a bridge 1.8km outside the city, Dresden was stripped of its world heritage status, yet Edinburgh is being trashed wholesale, and nothing is done. Why, when an entire range of listed historic buildings in St Andrew Square was ripped down without an Environmental Impact Assessment as required by law, did Unesco do nothing? […]

So what has Unesco world heritage status done for us?

Juxtaposition – the fact of two things being seen or placed close together with contrasting effect
Anodyne – not likely to cause offence or disagreement and somewhat dull

Sample Unit 3

Reading and Writing: Argumentation, Persuasion and Instructional

Section A Reading: 40 marks

In the separate Resource Material there are five texts on the theme of 'Holidays at home' labelled Texts A–E. Read each text carefully and answer all the questions below that relate to each of the texts.

Text A

| A 14 | How many people in total were employed in tourism jobs in 2013? | [1] |

| A 15 | How much money will the UK tourism industry be worth in 2025? | [1] |

| A 16 | How many more tourism jobs will there be in 2025 compared to 2013? | [1] |

Text B

A 17 Tick the box that best describes the purpose of this text: [1]

(a) Personal use ☐

(b) Public use ☐

(c) Occupational use ☐

(d) Educational use ☐

A 18 The writer uses the term 'staycation'. Which of the following definitions best describes what staycation means? [1]

(a) The place where you stay while on holiday ☐

(b) When you decide to stay in a hostel rather than a hotel ☐

(c) A holiday spent in your home country rather than abroad ☐

(d) A new holiday resort for tourists ☐

(e) When you leave someone behind when going on holiday ☐

A 19 Text B gives 'Tips for a successful staycation'. Put these tips into a logical order (1–4) for those wishing to take a staycation. One answer has been completed for you.

- Buy any tickets or passes in advance. ☐

- When you have discovered what is available make a rough plan. ☐

- Research what you can do in your local area. ☐

- When taking your staycation do not answer work emails or phone calls. [4] [3]

Text C

A 20 Explain what the Family Holiday Association can do. **[1]**

A 21 How do specialist tour operators make sure there is a
wide range of accessible holiday options for wheelchair users? **[2]**

Text D

A 22 Text D states that the cost of a holiday at home was 'negligible'.
Tick the box that best describes what this word means. **[1]**

(a) Negative ☐

(b) Very small ☐

(c) Expensive ☐

(d) Valuable ☐

A 23 What impression do you get of Amanda Moore? Why do you
get this impression? **[5]**

A 24 Summarize what Amanda Moore and her family did during their staycation. **[5]**

Text E

A 25 How does the writer persuade you to visit Pembrokeshire? **[8]**

Refer to the language used by the writer to influence the reader.

A 26 Compare what the writers of Texts D and E say about what
makes a perfect holiday. **[10]**

You must make it clear from which text you get your information.

Section B Writing: 40 marks

*In this section you will be assessed for the quality of your **writing** skills.*

10 marks are awarded for communication and organization; 10 marks are awarded for writing accurately.

You should aim to write between 200–300 words.

B1. Write a leaflet persuading people to visit a tourist destination of your choice.

Write your leaflet. **[20]**

B1. Text D mentions 'plonking the children in front of *CBeebies*'.
Give your ideas and views on how parents should entertain their young children.

Write your article. **[20]**

Reading and Writing: Argumentation, Persuasion and Instructional

Resource materials

Text A gives UK tourism statistics.

9.6%
of total UK jobs

3.1m
total jobs in 2013

9%
of UK GDP

£126.9bn
UK GDP in 2013

...and has been a major **job creator**

173,000
net increase in jobs
2010-12 (4.7% p.a.)

1/3
of all sector UK net
increase in jobs 2010-12

Tourism is predicted to grow...

+6%
international
demand
growth p.a.

+1.5%
outbound
demand
growth p.a.

+3%
domestic
demand
growth p.a.

...and be **worth**

£257.4bn
by 2025

providing...

jobs

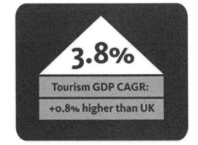
+630,000
more tourism jobs

9.9%
UK GDP

3.8%
Tourism GDP CAGR:
+0.8% higher than UK

Text B gives tips for a successful 'staycation'.

> Buy any tickets or passes in advance. This will help to make sure that your staycation remains stress free.

> When you have discovered what is available then you should make a rough plan. A plan will help to make sure you get the right balance during your time off.

> When taking your staycation make sure that you do not answer work emails or phonecalls. Your staycation needs to be a relaxing break after all.

> Research what you can do in your local area. Find out as much as you can about facilities and costs.

Text C is an article about accessible holidays for all.

Accessible Holidays At Home or Abroad

Everybody needs a break from time to time; even just a few days in a new environment can make all the difference – but it is important to get the details right if you are to get the best out of it.

If your family is on a low income, and cannot afford a holiday, help may be available from organisations like the Family Holiday Association. If you haven't had a break for at least four years, then ask to be referred by your GP, social worker or health visitor.

For families with disabled children, the government has passed an amendment to the Children and Young People Bill, which places a positive duty on local authorities to ensure availability of short breaks (this used to be known as respite care). All local authorities must meet this requirement, and since 2008, funding and guidance has been provided to ensure that it is achieved. The Local Authority must promote information about the short breaks that are available, and how they decide to allocate them.

There is a wide range of accessible holiday options for wheelchair users and others with reduced mobility or other special needs. From city breaks to beach resorts around the world, as well as luxurious cruises, there are specialist operators who make sure that the destinations have been inspected, so that you can be confident about the level of access and facilities available.

Text D is an article about taking a holiday at home.

Last week a survey revealed that more than one in three of us now stay at home for our holidays. Julia Llewellyn Smith meets the 'staycationers'.

Last summer, Amanda Moore's busy schedule meant that she delayed booking her summer holiday.

At the last minute, Mrs Moore, a nurse, discovered the perfect property: a four-bedroom, three-bathroom house with a sunny garden. It was within walking distance of shops and historic attractions but a short drive to the countryside and coast. Childcare was included and, astonishingly, the cost was negligible. This holiday would involve no 6am departures from chaotic airports, no meltdowns at the discovery they'd forgotten the toddler's favourite stuffed elephant or that the supermarket only sold UHT milk.

Mrs Moore from Bath had decided to embrace the latest holiday trend: taking a holiday in one's own home. Last week *Travel Weekly* published a survey showing that 38 per cent of 2,000 Britons were planning not to go away at all this year but to spend any annual leave at home.

"My husband and I were full of excitement," recalls Mrs Moore. "Our babysitter was available and we never can afford childcare abroad. He and I were going to visit all the city's sights, go to the cinema in the afternoon, have long, boozy lunches in great restaurants. I was going to read my way through a pile of classic books and enjoy all sorts of spa visits. On the babysitter's day off we were going to take the children on a day trip. I thought we would save lots of money and get a refreshing new perspective on surroundings we took for granted."

But for the Moores, a more humdrum experience awaited. "Just before our staycation we'd had a home office built in the garden," says Mrs Moore. "We decided to spend a day moving our things into it. This expanded into the entire holiday as we had lots of problems installing broadband.

"One day it was hailing, so we ended up plonking the children in front of *CBeebies*, while I caught up with the ironing. The other day we went to Legoland. It cost nearly £150 just to get in, without meals and our youngest vomited all over the car on the way home. We didn't go to a single gallery or film, and the only meal out we had was a family excursion to Pizza Hut when the Tesco delivery man failed to show.

"My husband kept disappearing to check emails. I got in a bad mood because all of the time at home made me woefully aware of how shabby the decor was and how we couldn't afford to do it up. I was permanently stressed about an ongoing row with the neighbours about their hedges. If we'd gone away I'd have escaped from all that – though I'd have been worrying about money instead."

Text E is taken from a travel brochure persuading people to visit Pembrokeshire.

Visit Pembrokeshire

Known across the world for its awesome coastal scenery, protected by Britain's only coastal National Park, Pembrokeshire is the perfect holiday destination: golden sands backed by towering cliffs teeming with wildlife and a 186 mile coastal path that leads you on an adventure around our coastline.

In this, our Year of Adventure 2016 why not have yourself that adventure, the one that always gets put off? Now is the time to be bold, to try new things, to conquer a new challenge. We all need a little adventure in our lives.

Adventures come in all shapes and sizes. There's the full blown heart racing, adrenalin filled, action packed type like coasteering, kayaking, climbing or diving or an adventure can be a child's first foray into a rock pool, the first time you put paint to a canvas or sample new food. They're all adventures.

Families have no end of choice; adventure parks, castles and boat trips, they are just some of the attractions and events that will create lasting memories that are talked about for years.

And when the fresh air gets the better of you and it's time to rest your head, you can retire to your accommodation of choice; a seaside hotel, cosy country cottage or something more unusual, knowing that in the morning you can do it all again.

If you've always wanted to 'give it go' now is the time; a family holiday, active break, day out or short break. You'll find *your* adventure in Pembrokeshire.

http://www.visitpembrokeshire.com/

Glossary

Chronological the order in which things occurred

Context the words that come before and after a particular word or phrase and help clarify its meaning; the circumstances or background against which something happens

Continuous text text written in sentences and paragraphs

Evaluate to form an idea of the state or value of something

Fact a thing that is known to have happened and/or to be true

Inference a conclusion you reach based on evidence and reasoning

Logical correctly reasoned

Non-continuous text text which presents information in other ways, for example charts, tables, diagrams and graphs

Opinion a personal view or judgement formed about something, not necessarily based on fact or knowledge

Purpose the purpose of a text is what the writer deliberately sets out to achieve. They may wish to persuade, encourage, advise or even anger their reader, or a mixture of these

Scan a reading technique that consists of looking quickly through a text to find specific details, rather than reading it closely to take in all the information

Sequence arrange in a particular order

Subjective based on or influenced by personal feelings, tastes or opinions

Summary a brief document or statement that gives the main points of something. It is a shortened version of a longer text which is written up in the reader's own words. Producing a summary tests your understanding of what you have read

Synonym a word that means the same thing or something very similar

Synthesize to form something by bringing together information from different sources

Tone manner of expression that shows the writer's attitude, for example, an apologetic or angry tone

Topic sentence often the first sentence in a paragraph, it tells the reader what the paragraph is about, and is followed by other sentences which give more detail

Verbal reasoning skills which help you understand and comprehend information, like reason and deduction